OPNET LAB MANUAL TO ACCOMPANY

DATA AND COMPUTER COMMUNICATIONS
SEVENTH EDITION

AND

COMPUTER NETWORKING WITH INTERNET PROTOCOLS AND TECHNOLOGY
FOUTH EDITION
BY **WILLIAM STALLINGS**

KEVIN BROWN AND
LEANN CHRISTIANSON

PEARSON
Prentice
Hall

Upper Saddle River, NJ 07458

Vice President and Editorial Director, ECS: *Marcia J. Horton*
Senior Acquisitions Editor: *Alan Apt*
Associate Editor: *Sarah E. Parker*
Editorial Assistant: *Patrick Lindner*
Vice President and Director of Production and Manufacturing, ESM: *David W. Riccardi*
Executive Managing Editor: *Vince O'Brien*
Managing Editor: *Camille Trentacoste*
Production Editor: *Mary C. Massey*
Director of Creative Services: *Paul Belfanti*
Creative Director: *Carole Anson*
Cover Designer: *Daniel Sandin*
Manufacturing Manager: *Trudy Pisciotti*
Manufacturing Buyer: *Ilene Kahn*
Executive Marketing Manager: *Pamela Hersperger*
Marketing Assistant: *Barrie Reinhold*

© 2005 Pearson Education, Inc.
Pearson Prentice Hall
Pearson Education, Inc.
Upper Saddle River, NJ 07458

The author and publisher of this book have used their best efforts in preparing this book. These efforts include the development, research, and testing of the theories and programs to determine their effectiveness. The author and publisher make no warranty of any kind, expressed or implied, with regard to these programs or the documentation contained in this book. The author and publisher shall not be liable in any event for incidental or consequential damages in connection with, or arising out of, the furnishing, performance, or use of these programs.

Printed in the United States of America

10 9 8 7 6 5 4 3 2 1

ISBN: 0-13-148252-1

Pearson Education Ltd., *London*
Pearson Education Australia Pty. Ltd., *Sydney*
Pearson Education Singapore, Pte. Ltd.
Pearson Education North Asia Ltd., *Hong Kong*
Pearson Education Canada, Inc., *Toronto*
Pearson Educación de Mexico, S.A. de C.V.
Pearson Education—Japan, *Tokyo*
Pearson Education Malaysia, Pte. Ltd.
Pearson Education, Inc., *Upper Saddle River, New Jersey*

Lab 0   Getting Started with OPNET IT Guru Academic Edition

Overview

OPNET IT Guru Academic Edition provides network modeling, simulation, and analysis features. It provides the user with the ability to choose network devices, such as switches, routers, and workstations; connect them together with various types of links, such as Ethernet 100BaseT, FDDI, and ATM; and define network traffic patterns. OPNET may then be used to simulate the behavior of the modeled network, to collect statistics, such as application response time or link utilization, and to display graphs of the collected statistics. OPNET may also be used to design computer networks from scratch, to validate or troubleshoot an existing configuration, or to evaluate a proposed upgrade.

Objective

To learn the basics required to use OPNET effectively, including creating projects, building models, choosing statistics, managing scenarios, and viewing results.

Install OPNET IT Guru Academic Edition

Before downloading the software, make sure that your system conforms to the minimum system requirements for running IT Guru Academic Edition.

System Requirements

Operating Systems:
> Windows XP (Service Pack 1 is required.)
> Windows 2000 (Service Packs 1 and 2 are supported but not required.)
> Windows NT 4.0 (Service Packs 3, 5, and 6a are supported. Service Packs 4 and 6 are not supported.)

Memory:
> 256 MB is required.

Disk Space:
> 200 MB is required. An additional 200 MB is required during installation only. An additional 20 MB is suggested for storing models created during lab exercises.

Display:
> 1024 x 768 resolution or higher is required. 256 or more colors are required.

To begin the installation process, visit the IT Guru Academic Edition website at
http://www.opnet.com/services/university/itguru_academic_edition.html

Click on **Download Now**.

You will then be asked to register with OPNET so that an account may be created for you. When this step has been completed, a login and password will be emailed to you together with the web address of the download site.

When you receive your login and password, download the application and follow the installation and license management instructions.

Launching OPNET IT Guru Academic Edition

Select the **Start** button => **OPNET IT Guru Academic Edition x.x** => **OPNET IT Guru Academic Edition** (where **x.x** is the release number).

Read the license agreement and, if you agree with the statement, click on the **I have read this SOFTWARE AGREEMENT and I understand and accept the terms and conditions described herein** button. The main OPNET window will appear.

OPNET IT Guru Academic Edition provides two tutorials to help you get acquainted with OPNET. The first one, the Introduction, leads you through the various OPNET features, including the Project Editor, Toolbars, and the Workspace. The second, Small Internetworks, guides you through the creation and simulation of a local area network (LAN) model.

Click on the **Help** tab => **Tutorial**. OPNET will spawn off a PDF viewer so that you may page through the tutorials. Under **Basic Lessons**, click on the **Introduction** button and read through the document. When you are done, close your PDF viewer window.

Tutorials

Basic Lessons

1 Introduction (10 minutes)

2 Small Internetworks (1 hour)

☛ Troubleshooting Tutorial Simulations

Click on the **Help** tab => **Tutorial**. Under **Basic Lessons**, click on the **Small Internetworks** button. As you read through the document, perform the described actions using OPNET. You will model a small LAN, identify statistics to be collected, and view the results of the simulation. While completing the tutorial, you will learn to perform many of the tasks that will be required in later lab exercises, including duplicating scenarios, comparing results between scenarios, and using the Rapid Configuration tool. When you have completed the tutorial, close your PDF viewer window.

You should now be ready to complete any of the lab exercises included in this manual.

Questions

1. While completing the Small Internetworks tutorial, record the following values:
    a)   Peak load for the first_floor scenario.

    b)   Maximum delay for the first_floor scenario.

    c)   The elapsed time it took to run the simulation for the first_floor scenario.

2. Explain the difference between **Elapsed Time** and **Simulated Time**. In the Single Floor scenario, which was larger? Explain why.

3. What is the average Ethernet load in the expansion scenario? What is the utilization of the Ethernet LAN? Remember that the utilization is the load divided by the network capacity (both measured in bits/second).

4. What was the elapsed time when running the expansion scenario? Was it longer than the elapsed time for the first_floor scenario? If so, why?

Lab 1   Shared Ethernet Networks

Overview

In a shared Ethernet network, end systems are typically connected together using a **hub**. The hub retransmits any incoming frames on all outgoing lines creating a single **broadcast domain** for all the devices. Within this domain, the **Carrier Sense Multiple Access with Collision Detection** (CSMA/CD) MAC protocol is used to determine which node may transmit at any given time and to resolve **collisions** if two or more nodes transmit at the same time.

Objective

To determine the throughput of a shared Ethernet network under load.

Build the Simulation Model

Start up OPNET IT Guru Academic Edition.
Select the **File** tab => **New...**
Choose **Project** and click on **OK**.
Change the **Project Name** to **Shared_Ethernet**. Change the **Scenario Name** to **Low_Load**, and click on **OK**.
In the **Initial Topology** window, select **Create Empty Scenario** and click on **Next**.
In the **Choose Network Scale** window, select **Office** and click on **Next**.
In the **Specify Size** window, leave the parameters unchanged and click on **Next**.
In the **Select Technologies** window, scroll down and include the **ethernet** and **links** model families, and click on **Next**.
In the **Review** window, click on **OK**.

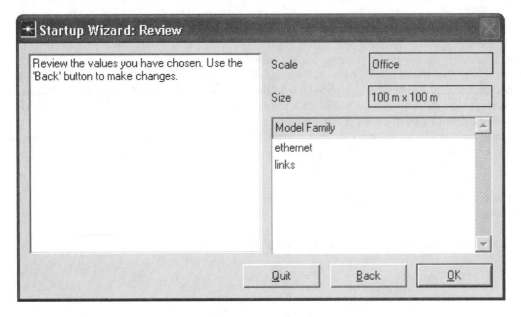

First, we will build a LAN in which the workstations are connected together with an Ethernet hub. An easy way to create a network with a large number of nodes in OPNET is to use the Rapid Configuration tool.

Select the **Topology** tab => **Rapid Configuration**. Set the **Configuration** to **Star** and click on **OK**. Set the **Center Node Model** to **ethernet16_hub**. Set the **Periphery Node Model** to **ethernet_station**. Set the **Link Model** to **10BaseT**. Set the **Number** to **12**, and click on **OK** to create the LAN.

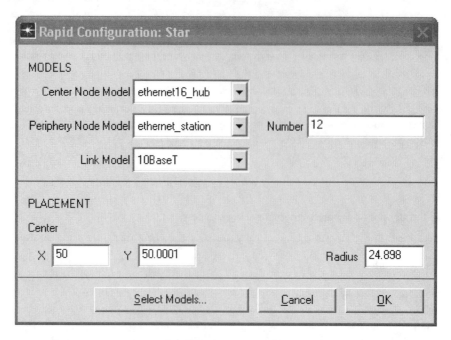

Right click on the hub (the device at the center of the star) and choose **View Node Description**. This device can support up to 16 Ethernet links at 10, 100, or 1000 Mbps. Note that the processing time within the device is considered to be zero, and that the hub retransmits incoming frames on all outgoing lines. Click on the close window icon to close the window. Right click on the hub and select **Set Name**. Set the **Name** to **Hub**. Click on **OK** to close the window.

Right click on one of the Ethernet stations and choose **View Node Description**. This device generates and receives Ethernet frames at configurable rates. Note that collision detection and resolution is handled by the hub. Click on the close window icon to close the window.

Now we need to set up the traffic patterns for the Ethernet stations. Right click on any of the stations and choose **Select Similar Nodes**. Next, right click on one of the stations and choose **Edit Attributes**. Put a check in the checkbox next to **Apply Changes to Selected Objects**. Expand the **Traffic Generation Parameters** and **Packet Generation Arguments** attributes. Set the **ON State Time** to **constant(1000)**, and the **OFF State Time** to **constant(0)**. This will ensure that the stations are always sending.
Set the **Interarrival Time (seconds)** to **exponential(0.004)** and the **Packet Size (bytes)** to **constant(100)**. Click on **OK** to apply the changes and close the window. Each station will now generate traffic at an average rate of one 100-byte packet every 4 milliseconds.

You can calculate the average traffic that each node will generate from the interarrival time and the packet size. For instance,

100 bytes/packet * 8 bits/byte * 1 packet/0.004 sec = 200 Kbps

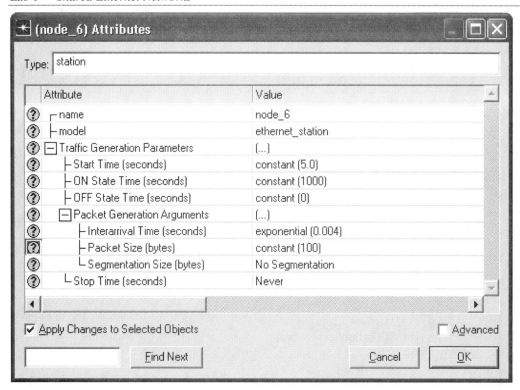

We are now done building the LAN model.

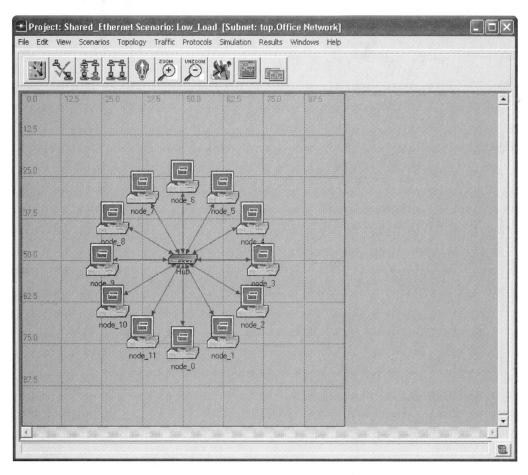

Configure the Simulation

Select the **Simulation** tab => **Choose Individual Statistics...**
Expand the **Global Statistics** item and the **Ethernet** item, and select the **Delay (sec)** statistic. Expand the **Traffic Sink** item and select the **Traffic Received (bits/sec)** statistic. Expand the **Traffic Source** item and select the **Traffic Sent (bits/sec)** statistic.
Expand the **Node Statistics** item and the **Ethernet** item, and select the **Collision Count**, **Load (bits/sec)**, **Traffic Forwarded (bits/sec)**, **Traffic Received (bits/sec)**, and **Utilization** statistics.
Click on **OK** to close the window.

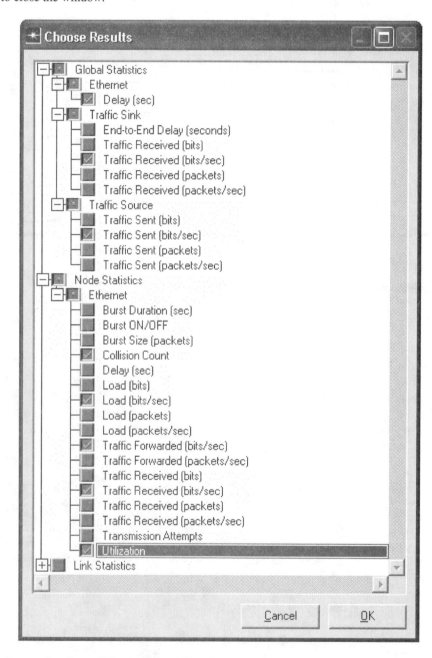

Select **Simulation** => **Configure Discrete Event Simulation...**
Under the **Common** tab, modify the **Duration** to **20** and the unit to **second(s)**.
Click on **OK** to close the window.

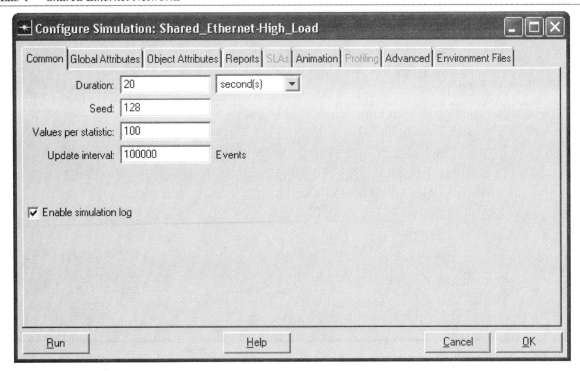

Duplicate the Scenario

Let us build another scenario in which each Ethernet station generates much more traffic. This will allow us to compare the performance of the LAN under different conditions.

Choose **Scenarios** => **Duplicate Scenario** and name the new scenario **High_Load**. Click on **OK** to create the scenario.

Right click on any of the stations and choose **Select Similar Nodes**. Next, right click on one of the stations and choose **Edit Attributes**. Put a check in the checkbox next to **Apply Changes to Selected Objects**. Expand the **Traffic Generation Parameters** and **Packet Generation Arguments** attributes. Set the **Interarrival Time (seconds)** to **exponential(0.001)**. Click on **OK** to apply the changes and close the window. Note that a shorter interarrival time means that packets will be generated more frequently.

Run the Simulation

Select the **Scenarios** tab => **Manage Scenarios...**
Edit the **Results** field in both rows and set the values to **<collect>** or **<recollect>**.
Click on **OK** to run both scenarios (one after the other).
When the simulation has completed, click on **Close** to close the window.

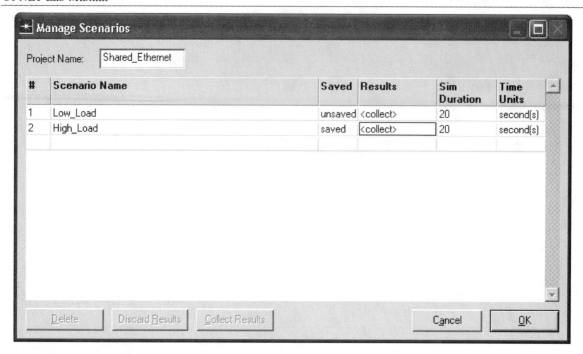

Inspect and Analyze Results

Select the **Scenarios** tab => **Switch to Scenario** and choose the **Low_Load** scenario.
Select the **Results** tab => **View Results…**

Select and expand the **Global Statistics** item and the **Traffic Source** item. Next, select the **Traffic Sent (bits/sec)** statistic. Also, expand the **Traffic Sink** item and select the **Traffic Received (bits/sec)** statistic. View all statistics in this lab exercise using **As Is** mode. For this level of load, the received bit rate is approximately equal to the sent bit rate. Click on the **Traffic Sent (bits/sec)** and **Traffic Received** (bits/sec) statistics again to disable the preview. Note that you may always click on **Show** for a more detailed graph than the preview provides.   Click on **Close** to close the **View Results** window.

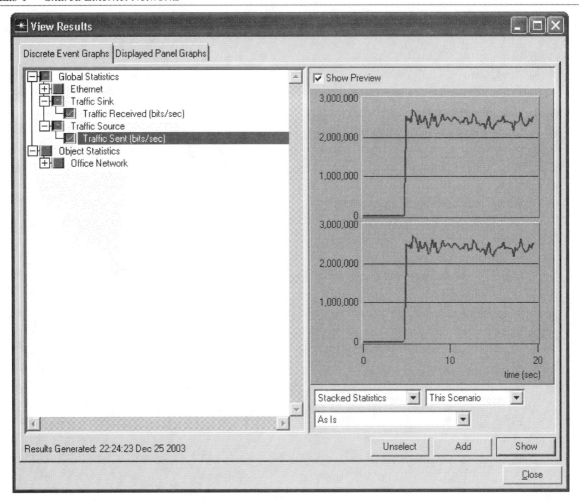

We will now examine the same statistics for the **High_Load** scenario. Repeat the previous steps including switching to the **High_Load** scenario, viewing results, and selecting statistics to view. In this case, you can see that much more traffic was sent than was received. The hub has become overloaded and cannot deliver all the traffic that it receives. Click on **Close** to close the **View Results** window.

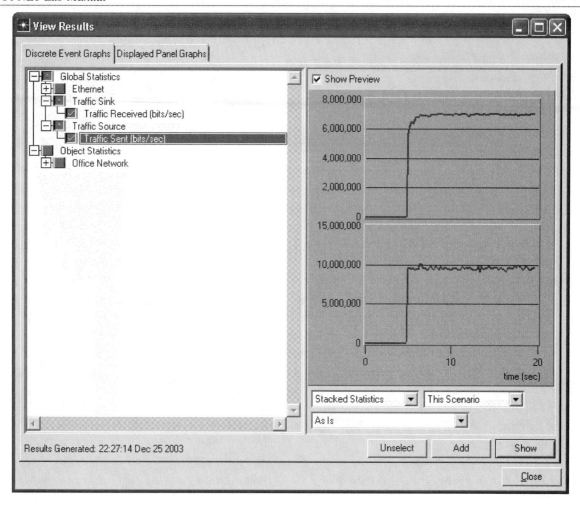

Let us compare results generated by the two scenarios.
Select the **Results** tab => **Compare Results…**

Select and expand the **Object Statistics** item, the **Office Network** item, the **node_0** item, and the **Ethernet** item. Select the **Load (bits/sec)** statistic and view in **As Is** mode. Click on **Show** for a more detailed graph. This statistic shows how much traffic was generated by this device. The measured values should approximately match the calculations we made earlier using the configuration parameters. Again, for the **Low_Load** scenario, 100 bytes/packet * 8 bits/byte * 1 packet/0.004 sec = 200 Kbps load per station. You may do a similar calculation for the **High_Load** scenario. Click on the close window icon and choose to **Delete** the panel to close the window. Click on the **Load (bits/sec)** statistic again to disable the preview.

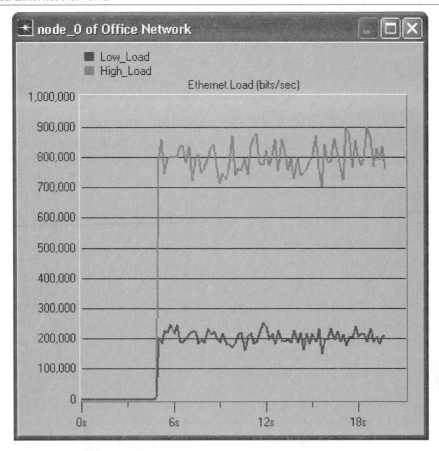

Discrepancies between the send and receive rates can be accounted for by inspecting the **Collision Count** statistic. Expand the **Hub** and the **Ethernet** items. Select the **Collision Count** statistic. Click on **Show** for a more detailed graph. Some of the packets that were sent collided and required retransmissions, reducing the throughput. This is true of both scenarios, but the **High_Load** scenario generated far more collisions. Click on the close window icon and **Delete** the panel. Click on the statistic again to disable the preview.

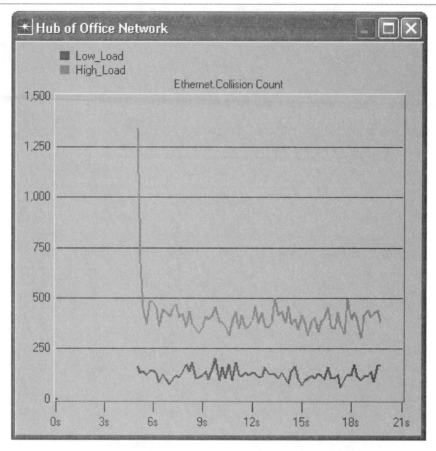

The hub's utilization can be viewed by selecting the **Utilization** statistic. Click on **Show** for a more detailed graph. The utilization essentially describes what percentage of the network's capacity is being used. Since 10BaseT links were used to connect the hub to the Ethernet stations, the capacity is 10 Mbps. You can see that the **High_Load** scenario traffic utilized a great deal more of the hub's capacity than the **Low_Load** scenario traffic. Click on the close window icon and **Delete** the panel. Click on the **Utilization** statistic again to disable the preview.

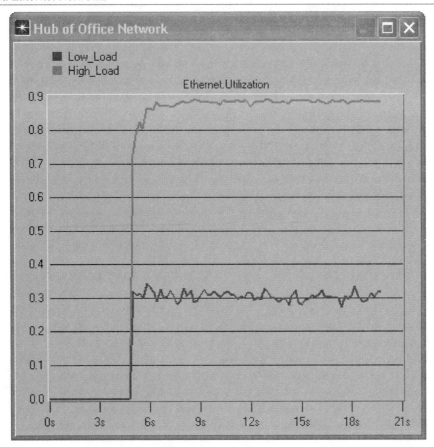

Lastly, expand the **Global Statistics** item and the **Ethernet** item, and select the **Delay (sec)** statistic. Click on **Show** for a more detailed graph. This statistic shows the delay experienced by all packets which have been successfully delivered. You can see that the delay is fairly consistent in the **Low-Load** scenario, but that the high level of traffic causes growing delays in the **High_Load** scenario. Click on the close window icon and **Delete** the panel. Click on **Close** to close the **Compare Results** window.

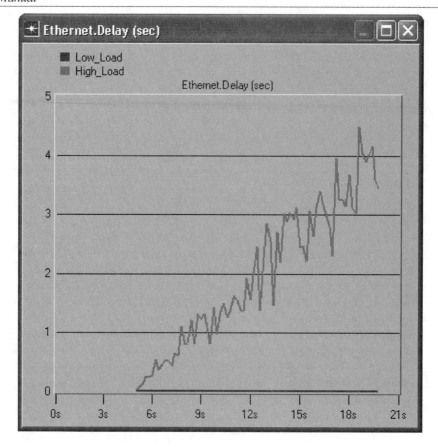

Save your model and close all windows.

Questions

1. Create several duplicate scenarios and modify the interarrival times for all the Ethernet stations to 0.0008, 0.002, 0.003, 0.005, and 0.006, respectively. Rerun the simulation, and record the **Traffic Received (bits/sec)** statistic for each scenario. Using a spreadsheet, plot the values, (together with the results you found in the preceding scenarios using interarrival times of 0.001 and 0.004). Find the interarrival time for which the maximum throughput is achieved. Calculate the offered load that corresponds to this interarrival time. Why does the throughput stop increasing even when the load is increased further?

2. Rerun the simulation using the same interarrival times in Question 1. For each run, record the **utilization** and **Traffic Received (bits/sec)**. Plot the values using a spreadsheet. How are the two statistics related? Why can't the system reach 100% utilization?

3. Some interactive applications require very short delay. Excessive load and resulting collisions can increase delay significantly. Modify the interarrival time and rerun the simulation to determine the **minimum** interarrival time and corresponding per-node load if the delay must be 0.005 second or less.

4. Modify the interarrival time and rerun the simulation to determine how large the interarrival time must be in order for the number of **collisions** per second to become negligible (less than 10 per second). What is the per-node load that corresponds to the interarrival time you found?

5. Under high loads, shared Ethernet LANs tend to perform poorly. Examine the **Delay** statistic for the **High_Load** scenario again. How does the delay experienced by packets change over the run of the simulation? Why does this behavior occur? What will happen to the delay if the load continues at the same level?

Lab 2   Switches versus Hubs

Overview

Ethernet hubs work at the physical layer, simply repeating any frames they receive on one port onto all other ports. For this reason, they are also called multiport repeaters. Switches, on the other hand, forward frames only to the port that is connected to the frame's destination. All the nodes connected to a hub are considered to be part of the same broadcast domain. In other words, any frame transmitted by one of the nodes will be received by all the rest. This configuration can limit throughput, as all nodes must share the capacity of the LAN. Since switches forward frames only on a single line, they create multiple broadcast domains, leading to great gains in throughput. The throughput of a switch is restricted, however, by its processing speed, the speed at which it can forward frames onto the correct outgoing link.

Objective

To examine the change in throughput in a local area network when upgrading from a hub to a switch.

Build the Simulation Model

Start up OPNET IT Guru Academic Edition.
Select the **File** tab => **New...**
Choose **Project** and click on **OK**.
Change the **Project Name** to **xx_Switch_vs_Hub** (where **xx** are your initials). Set the **Scenario Name** to **Hub** and click on **OK**.
In the **Initial Topology** window, select **Create Empty Scenario** and click on **Next**.
In the **Choose Network Scale** window, select **Office** and click on **Next**.
In the **Specify Size** window, accept the default values and click on **Next**.
In the **Select Technologies** window, include the **ethernet** and **ethernet_advanced** model families, and click on **Next**.
In the **Review** window, click on **OK**.

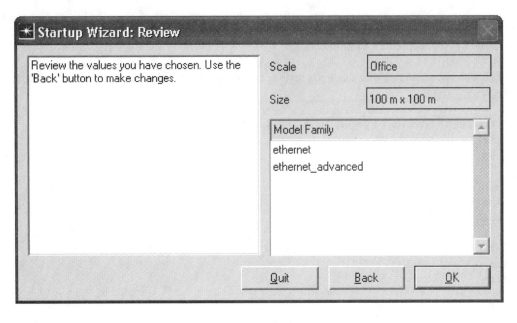

First, we will build a LAN in which the workstations are connected together with an Ethernet hub. An easy way to create a network with a large number of nodes in OPNET is with the Rapid Configuration tool.

Select the **Topology** tab => **Rapid Configuration**. Set the **Configuration** to **Star,** and click on **OK**. Set the **Center Node Model** to **ethernet16_hub**. Set the **Periphery Node Model** to **ethernet_station**. Set the **Link Model** to **10BaseT**. Set the **Number** to **12**, and click on **OK** to create the LAN.

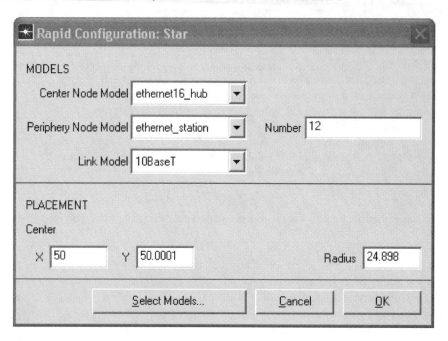

Right click on the hub and select **Set Name**. Set the **Name** to **Hub**. Click on **OK** to close the window.

Now we need to set up the traffic patterns for the Ethernet stations. Right click on any of the stations and choose **Select Similar Nodes**. Next, right click on one of the stations and choose **Edit Attributes**. Put a check in the checkbox next to **Apply Changes to Selected Objects**. Expand the **Traffic Generation Parameters** and **Packet Generation Arguments** attributes. Set the **ON State Time** to **constant(1000)**, and the **OFF State Time** to **constant(0)**. This will ensure that the stations are always sending.

Set the **Interarrival Time (seconds)** to **exponential(0.005)** and the **Packet Size (bytes)** to **constant(1000)**. Click on **OK** to apply the changes and close the window. Each station will now generate traffic at an average rate of one 1000-byte packet every 5 milliseconds.

You can calculate the average traffic that each node will generate from the interarrival time and the packet size. For instance,

1000 bytes/packet * 8 bits/byte * 1 packet/0.005 sec = 1.6 Mbps

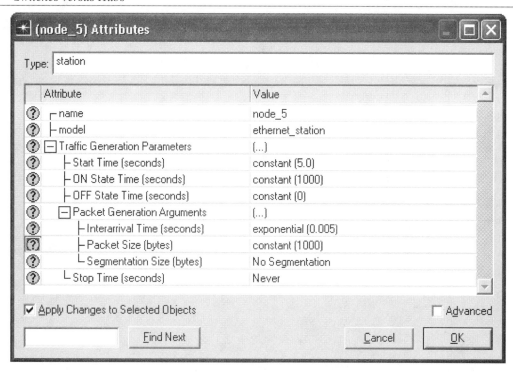

We are done creating the hub-based LAN. Your model should look like the one presented next.

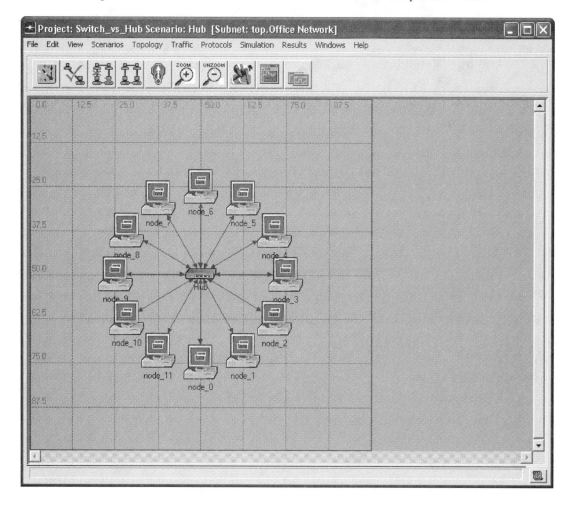

Configure the Simulation

Select the **Simulation** tab => **Choose Individual Statistics…**
Expand the **Global Statistics** item and the **Ethernet** item, and select the **Delay (sec)** statistic.
Expand the **Traffic Sink** item and select the **Traffic Received (bits/sec)** statistic. Expand the **Traffic Source** item and select the **Traffic Sent (bits/sec)** statistic.
Expand the **Node Statistics** item and the **Ethernet** item, and select the **Collision Count** statistic.
Click on **OK** to close window.

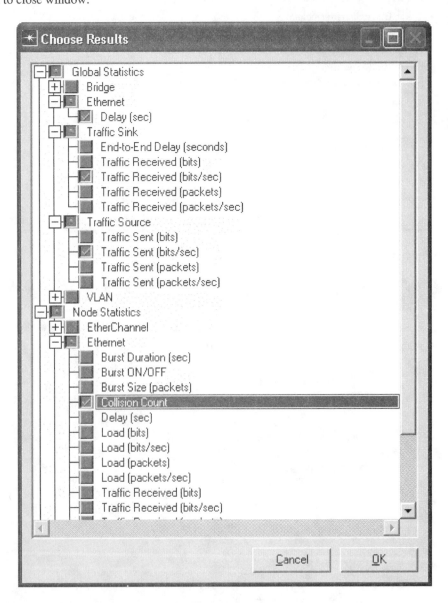

Select **Simulation** => **Configure Discrete Event Simulation…**
Under the **Common** tab, set the **Duration** to **2**, and the unit to **minute(s)**.
Click on **OK** to close the window.

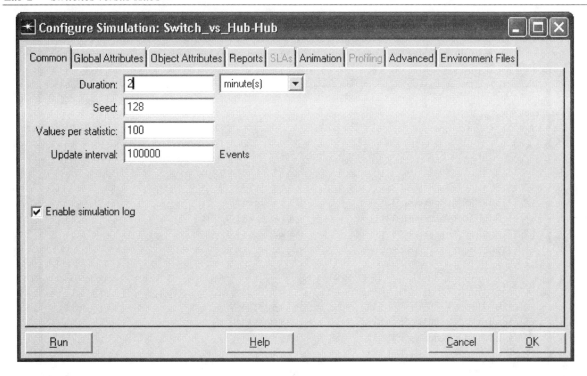

Duplicate the Scenario

Let us now build another scenario which uses an Ethernet switch as the center of the LAN instead of the hub. This will allow us to compare the performance of the two designs.

Choose **Scenarios => Duplicate Scenario**, and name the new scenario **Switch**. Click on **OK** to create the scenario.

Right click on the hub and choose **Edit Attributes**. Left click on the **model** attribute and choose **ethernet16_switch_adv** from the pull-down menu. Click on **OK** to make the change.

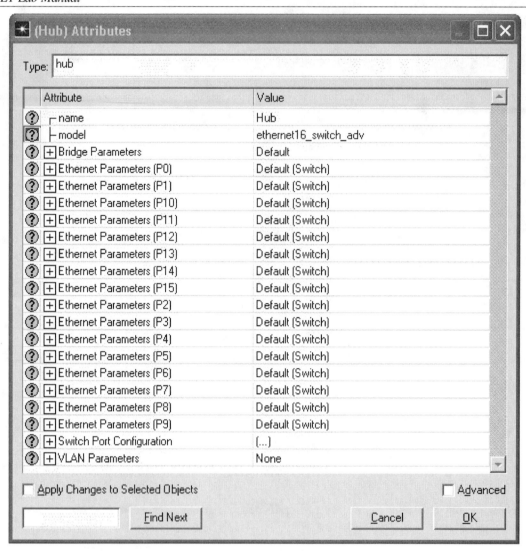

Right click on the switch and choose **Set Name**. Set the **Name** to **Switch** and click on **OK** to close the window.

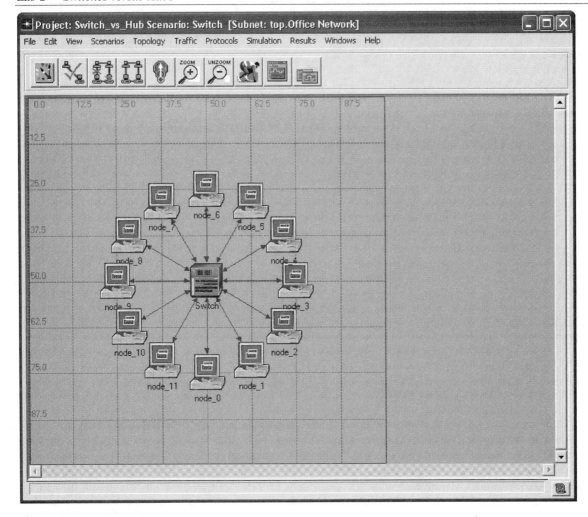

Run the Simulation

Select the **Scenarios** tab => **Manage Scenarios...**
Edit the **Results** field in both rows and set the values to **<collect>** or **<recollect>**.
Click on **OK** to run both scenarios (one after the other).
When the simulation has completed, click on **Close** to close the window.

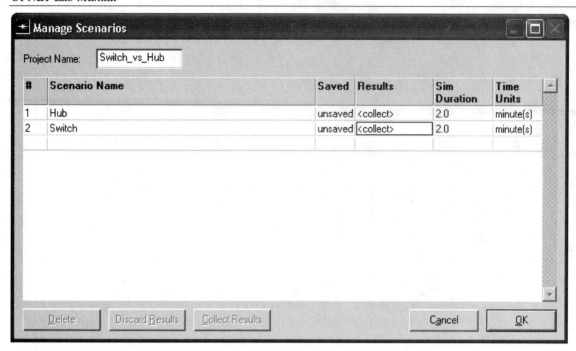

Inspect and Analyze Results

Select the **Results** tab => **Compare Results...**

Select and expand the **Global Statistics** item, and the **Ethernet** item and select the **Delay (sec)** statistic. View the statistic in **As Is** mode. Click on **Show** for a more detailed graph. This statistic shows the delivery delay for Ethernet frames. You can see that the delay for the switch scenario is small and constant, while the delay for the hub scenario is growing without bound. This is to be expected as we are loading the hub far past its capacity. Remember that we said each node was generating 1.6 Mbps of traffic. With 12 nodes in the system, that comes to 12 * 1.6 Mbps = 19.2 Mbps of offered load. The hub is operating at only 10 Mbps (since we specified 10BaseT links in the configuration). Click on the close window icon and **Delete** the panel. Click on the statistic again to disable the preview.

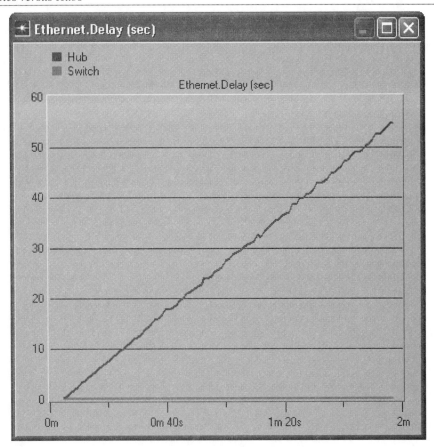

Expand the **Traffic Sink** item, and select the **Traffic Received (bytes/sec)** statistic. View the statistic in **As Is** mode. Click on **Show** for a more detailed graph. This statistic shows the sum total of traffic received by all stations in the LAN. You can see that the traffic received in the hub case tops out near 10 Mbps, the rated speed of the hub. The switch, on the other hand, easily delivers nearly twice that much traffic. Click on the close window icon and **Delete** the panel. Click on the statistic again to disable the preview.

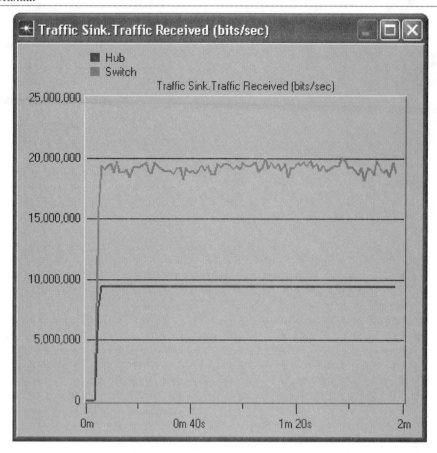

Expand the **Traffic Source** item, and select the **Traffic Sent (bytes/sec)** statistic. View the statistic in **As Is** mode. This statistic shows the sum total of traffic sent by all stations in the LAN. You can see that the same amount of traffic was generated in both scenarios. The switch, however, can actually carry this much traffic. Click on the statistic again to disable the preview. You can always click on **Show** for more detail.

Click on **Close** to close the **Compare Results** window.

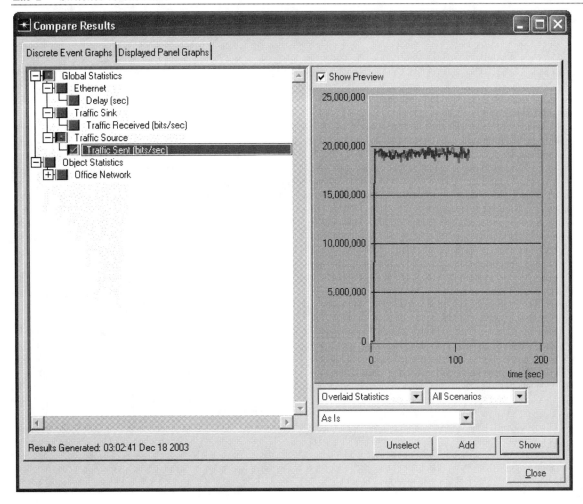

Lastly, we will look at a statistic which only applies to the hub scenario.

Select the **Scenarios** tab => **Switch to Scenario** and select the **Hub** scenario.
Select the **Results** tab => **View Results...**

Expand the **Object Statistics**, **Office Network**, **Hub**, and **Ethernet** items. Select the **Collision Count** statistic.
View the statistic in **As Is** mode. This statistic shows the number of collisions that occurred at the hub during the simulation.   You can see that close to 2000 collisions per second occurred. This is due to the heavy overloading of the hub.

Click on **Close** to close the **View Results** window.

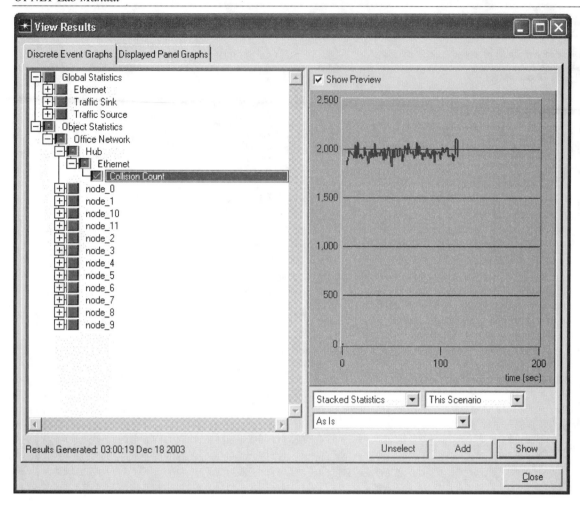

Save your model and close all windows.

Questions

1. The switching capacity of a switch determines the amount of load it can process. Duplicate the Switch scenario and name the new scenario **Switching_Speed**. Edit the switch and expand the **Bridge Parameters** attribute. Set the **Packet Service Rate (packets/sec)** attribute to **2000**. Now the switch can only handle 2000 frames per second. Calculate the number of packets generated (total) using the Packet Generation parameters of the Ethernet stations. Rerun the simulation and examine the Ethernet delay, Traffic Received, and Traffic Sent statistics. Explain your results.

2. Continue with the **Switching_Speed** scenario you created in Question 1. Determine how large **the Packet Service Rate** must be in order for the switch to handle all the offered load. In other words, how large must the rate be in order for the Traffic Received to equal the Traffic Sent? Explain your answer.

3. Duplicate the original Switch scenario and name the scenario **Smooth_Traffic**. Right click on one of the Ethernet stations and choose **Select Similar Objects**. Right click again on one of the Ethernet stations and choose **Edit Attributes**. Edit the **Packet Generation Parameters** and set the interarrival time to **constant(0.005)**. The average rate of traffic generation will be the same, but the frames will be generated regularly, rather than on the basis of an exponential (bursty) distribution. Rerun the simulation and compare your results to the Switch scenario results.

Lab 3   Routing Protocols

Overview
The Routing Information Protocol (RIP) is an example of a dynamic distance vector routing algorithm. This protocol chooses routes within a network that are of minimum distance. Routers adapt to changes in network topology (link or router failures) by exchanging information with their directly connected neighbors. Under normal conditions, routing table information is exchanged periodically (typically every 30 seconds). When changes in topology occur, however, the *triggered update* mechanism comes into play. If a router receives new routing information, it will wait 1–5 seconds (randomly determined) before passing that information on to its neighbors, rather than waiting the full 30 seconds. The triggered update mechanism causes topology information to propagate through the network much faster than it would using the standard timeout.

Objective
To simulate the behavior of several routers running the RIP routing protocol and to learn how to use routing tables to find paths in a network.

Build the Simulation Model

Start up OPNET IT Guru Academic Edition.
Select the **File** menu => **New...**
Choose **Project** and click on **OK**.
Change the **Project Name** to **xx_RIP_Network** (where **xx** are your initials) and click on **OK**.
In the **Initial Topology** window, select **Create Empty Scenario** and click on **Next**.
In the **Choose Network Scale** window, select **Logical** and click on **Next**.
In the **Select Technologies** window, click on **Next**.
In the **Review** window, click on **OK**.

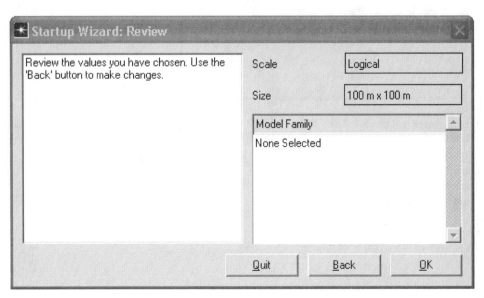

First, you may read the model usage guide for the RIP protocol. This guide explains how to configure nodes to use RIP and defines the meaning of each parameter.
Click on the **Protocols** tab => **RIP** => **Model Usage Guide**.
When you have finished reading the guide, click on the close window icon of the PDF viewer.

We will now build a small network of routers and set up the RIP parameters.

Select an **ethernet4_slip8_gtwy** object from the Object Palette and place it in the project workspace. Right click on the object and choose **View Node Description**. Note that this gateway is equipped with four Ethernet interfaces and eight SLIP interfaces. Click on the close window icon to close the window. Right click on the router, choose **Edit Attributes**, and set the **name** attribute to **Router1**. Expand the **RIP Parameters** attribute and the **Timers** attribute. Note that the **Update Interval (seconds)** is set to 30 seconds. This means that a router will exchange its routing table with each of its neighbors every 30 seconds, even if new information is not learned. Click on **OK** to close the window.

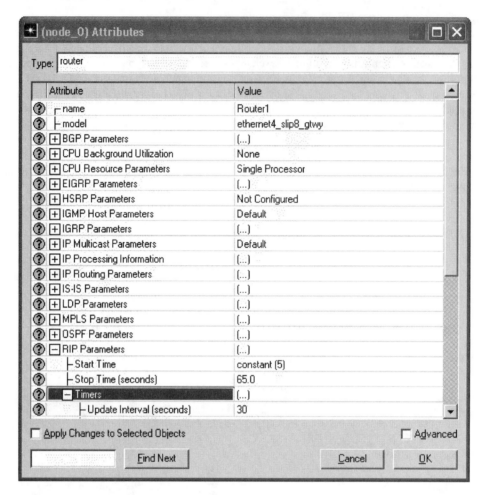

Left click on the router and choose **Copy** from the **Edit** menu at the top of the window. Choose **Paste** from the **Edit** menu five times to generate five copies of the first router in the project workspace. Arrange them in a circle and then connect them together into a ring using six **PPP_DS1** lines from the Object Palette. Each router should be connected to two other routers.

Paste two more routers on the map. Using 2 more **PPP_DS1** lines, make a tail off of Router6. Your final network should look like a ring of six routers with a tail of two routers:

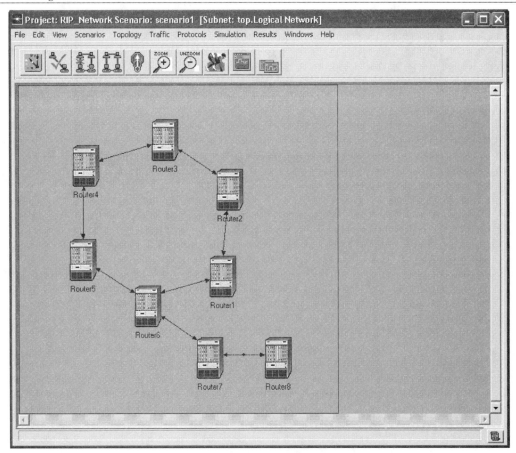

Select the **Protocols** menu => **IP** => **Routing** => **Configure Routing Protocols...** Check the boxes next to **RIP, Apply the above selection to subinterfaces**, and **Visualize Routing Domains.** Select the radio button next to **All interfaces (including loopback).** Click on **OK** to close the window. By doing so, you have ensured that the RIP routing protocol will be used to route packets across all the interfaces on all the routers. Note that the legend shows that RIP is used on all links.

Now we are going to configure one of the PPP links to fail part of the way through the simulation. Select **utilities** from the pull-down menu in the Object Palette in order to display all utility objects. Place a **Failure Recovery** object in the project workspace. Right click on the failure object and **Edit Attributes**. Set the **name** to **Link Failure**. Expand the **Link Failure/Recovery Specification** attribute and set **rows** to **1**. Expand **row 0**, and set the **Name** to **Logical Network.Router 1<->Router 6**. Set the **Time** to **300**. Note that the **Status** is set to **Fail**. This failure node will cause the link between router 1 and router 6 to fail 300 seconds into the simulation. Click on **OK** to close the window.

Configure and Run the Simulation

Select the **Simulation** tab => **Choose Individual Statistics...**
Expand the **Global Statistics** item, and the **RIP** item and select the **Traffic Received (bits/sec)** statistic. Right click on the statistic and choose **Change Collection Mode.** Check the box next to **Advanced**, and change the **Capture Mode** to **all values.** This will ensure that OPNET will provide a more detailed graph.
Click on **OK** twice to close the windows.

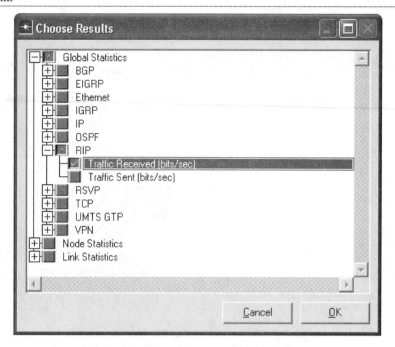

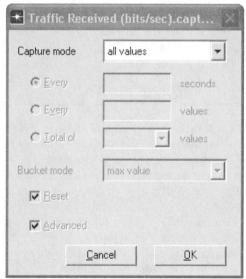

Select **Simulation => Configure Discrete Event Simulation...**

Under the **Common** tab, set the **Duration** to **10**, and the unit to **minute(s)**.

Click on the **Global Attributes** tab. Set the **IP Interface Addressing Mode** to **Auto Address/Export**. Set the **IP Routing Table Export/Import** field to **Export**. This will cause the routing tables of all the routers to be written to a text file when the simulation completes. Set the **RIP Sim Efficiency** to **disabled**. Set the **RIP Stop Time** to **10000**. This will ensure that the routers keep exchanging routing information even when their routing tables have stabilized.

Click on **Run** to run the simulation.

When the simulation has completed, click on **Close** to close the window.

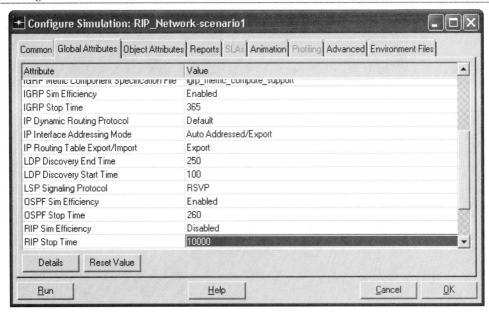

Inspect and Analyze Results

Select **Results => View Results...**

Select and expand the **Global Statistics** item and the **RIP** item, and select the **Traffic Received (bits/sec)** statistic. This statistic shows how much traffic was generated by the routing algorithm. Click on **Show** to generate a separate window for the statistics graph. You should see nice, regular peaks in routing protocol traffic every 30 seconds except for two periods, one at the beginning of the simulation and one half way through. Select the first 2 minutes of the graph to zoom in. You should now be able to see that many irregularly timed updates were done very quickly at the beginning of the simulation. These updates are due to the triggered update mechanism in RIP. The other period of irregular updates is due to the link failure that occurred after 300 seconds. Click on the close window icon and **Delete** the panel. Click on **Close** to close the **View Results** window.

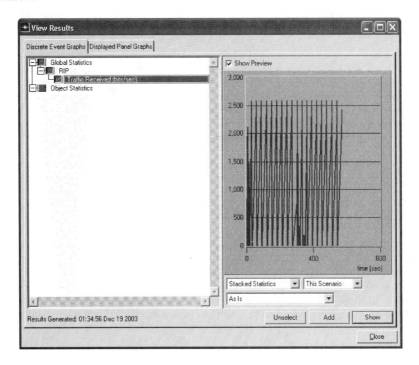

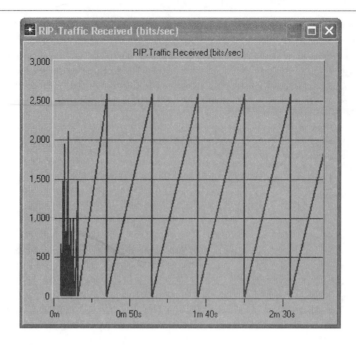

Select **Scenarios => Duplicate Scenario...** Accept the default scenario name of **scenario2** by clicking on the **OK** button. Left click on the Failure node to select it and choose **Edit => Cut** to remove the Failure node. Choose **Simulation => Run Discrete Event Simulation** to generate results for this scenario in which no link failures occur. When the simulation has completed, click on **Close** to close the window.

Select **File => Model Files => Refresh Model Directories.** Select **File => Open...** Choose to open a **Generic Data File**, and from the list displayed, choose **xx_RIP_Network-scenario2-ip_addresses**. This file shows the IP addresses and subnetwork masks which have been assigned to each interface by OPNET. Note that each router has one interface called the *loopback* interface that is not attached to any link. These logical interfaces are commonly used for testing or to allow two socket programs to communicate even if they are running on the same machine. Note that the figure below shows only part of the entire file. Click on the close window icon to close the addresses window.

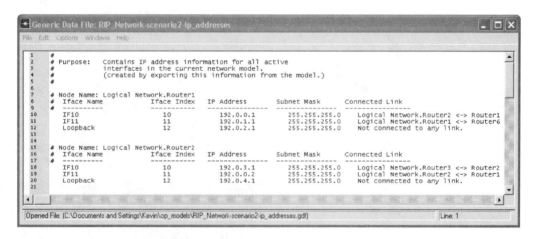

Now we will inspect the routing tables of the nodes. Select **File => Open...** Choose to open a **Generic Data File** again, and from the list displayed, choose **xx_RIP_Network-scenario2-ip_routes**. This file is a dump of the routing tables maintained at each router in the state they were in at the end of the simulation run. There are two parts to the file. In the first part, the directly connected networks for each router are listed. A network is directly connected to a router if the router has an interface which matches that network address up to the length of the subnetwork mask. For example, Router1 has an interface of 192.0.2.1 with a subnetwork mask of 255.255.255.0. A subnetwork mask of 255.255.255.0 requires that the first 24 bits of the IP address match the network address. So the 192.0.2.0 network matches the interface address of 192.0.2.1 and Router1 is directly connected to the 192.0.2.0 network.

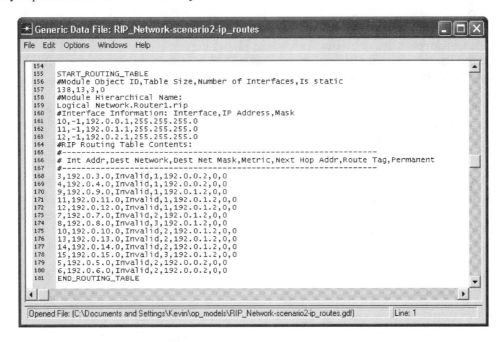

The second part of the ip_routes file shows routes to networks which are *not* directly connected. Note that the next figure below shows just the part of the routing table file which applies to Router1. Your file will include one routing table for each router. Note that your address assignments may be different, depending on the order in which you placed the routers in the workspace.

Using the **ip_routes** file, we can determine the path that a packet would take through our network. Let's say that we would like to find the path from **Router1** to **Router8**. Using the **xx_RIP_Network-scenario1-ip_addresses** file, let's pick an interface on each router (other than the loopback interfaces).

Router1: 192.0.1.1
Router8: 192.0.13.2

192.0.13.2 is on the 192.0.13.0 network so that is what we'll be looking for in the routing tables. Note that, in order to reduce the size of the routing tables, routing is done based on network addresses rather than individual IP addresses.

Starting with Router1's routing table, we look for the destination network (**Dest Network** field in the table), 192.0.13.0, and pull out the **Next Hop Addr** field. In this case, the **Next Hop Addr** is 192.0.1.2. We now look at the **Interface Information** portion of this file or in the **xx_RIP_Network-scenario1-ip_addresses** file to see which router has an interface with this address. In this case, it is Router6. We then repeat our steps, first looking for the destination network, 192.0.13.0, in Router6's routing table, pulling out the next hop address (192.0.11.2), and finding the router that owns this address (Router7). We continue until we reach a router that is directly connected to the destination network. Router 7 has an interface (192.0.13.1) on the destination network, meaning that it has a direct connection to Router8 (192.0.13.2). You can see that Router7 and Router8 are on the same network because their IP addresses are the same up to the length of the subnetwork mask (24 bits).

In our example, the path is

Router1 (192.0.1.1) => Router6 (192.0.1.2) => Router7 (192.0.11.2) => Router8 (192.0.13.2) Success!

Click on the close window icon to close the **ip_routes** window.

You may also access the routing table dump file directly. Using Windows Explorer, look in your home directory for a directory called **op_models**. Change to this directory and look for the generic data file called **xx_RIP_Network-scenario1-ip_routes.gdf**. This is the file you just inspected from within OPNET. If you have trouble finding the directory, select **Edit => Preferences**, and look for the **mod_dirs** attribute. The associated value is the path to your **op_models** directory.

Save your model and close all windows.

Questions

1. Look at the **ip_addresses** and **ip_routes** files associated with the first scenario (scenario1), in which a failure occurred on the line which connects Router1 and Router6. You can switch between scenarios by choosing **Scenarios => Switch to Scenario**. Find the path from Router1 to Router8 as shown above.

2. Write a program which takes three parameters, a source IP address, a destination IP address, and the **ip_routes** file from the model you created above. Your program must automate the process of finding the path from the source to the destination. You must print out output as shown above. For example:

RouterA (interface x.x.x.x) => RouterB (interface y.y.y.y) =>... Success/Failure

3. Duplicate scenario1 and add another row to the Failure Recovery object so that the link between Router6 and Router5 fails at time = 300 seconds. Rerun the simulation and examine the **ip_routes** file. Is there a path from Router1 to Router8? If so, what is it? If not, why not?

Lab 4   Frame Relay Network Performance

Overview
Frame Relay is a connection-oriented, unreliable technology based on virtual circuits. A virtual circuit must be set up between a source and destination before any data may be exchanged. Most Frame Relay service providers support Permanent Virtual Circuits (PVC), which are long-lived connections, as opposed to Switched Virtual Circuits (SVC), which are set up at call time. When a PVC is set up, certain parameters which govern the behavior of the PVC are agreed upon. These include the Committed Information Rate (CIR), committed burst rate (Bc), and the excess burst rate (Be). The CIR is the rate (in bits per second) which the service provider guarantees to the customer. The committed burst rate specifies how quickly that data may be sent. For instance, a customer may contract for a CIR of 64 Kbps, and a Bc of 32 Kbits/100 ms. In this case, the customer may send 64 Kbits per second, but no more than 32 Kbits in any 100 ms period. Frame Relay service providers will accept additional data above the CIR and transmit it if there is excess capacity in the network at that time. The amount of excess data that they will carry is defined by the excess burst rate. Any data frames that are sent in excess of the CIR are marked with the Discard Eligible bit set. These frames are discarded first in the event of congestion.

Objective
To examine the behavior of a Frame Relay PVC as contract parameters are varied.

Build the Simulation Model

Start up OPNET IT Guru Academic Edition.

First, it would be useful to read the information provided by OPNET regarding Frame Relay configuration.
Select the **File** tab => **Open**. Choose the **Frame_Relay** project and click on **OK**. Read through the Objective, Network Configuration, and Glossary pages.
Select **File** => **Close** when you are done.

Select the **File** tab => **New...**
Choose **Project** and click on **OK**.
Change the **Project Name** to **xx_WAN_Frame_Relay** (where **xx** are your initials). Set the **Scenario Name** to **CIR64** and click on **OK**.
In the **Initial Topology** window, select **Create Empty Scenario** and click on **Next**.
In the **Choose Network Scale** window, select **World** and click on **Next**.
In the **Choose Map** window, choose **usa** and click on **Next**.
In the **Select Technologies** window, scroll down and include the **frame_relay_advanced** model family, and then click on **Next**.
In the **Review** window, click on **OK**.

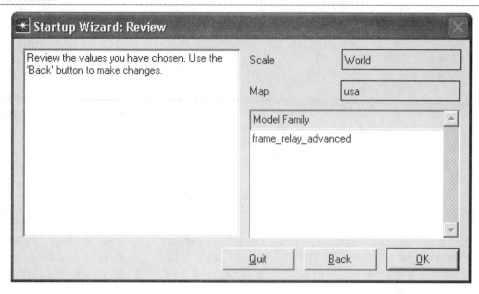

First, we will configure a bursty data application to generate traffic over our frame relay network. The File Transfer Protocol (FTP) will serve our purposes.

Select an **Application Config** object from the Object Palette and place it in the project workspace. Right click on the object and choose **Edit Attributes**. Set the **name** attribute to **Bursty Application**. Expand the **Application Definitions** attribute and set the **rows** attribute to **1**. Expand the **row 0** attribute and set the **Name** attribute to **FTP_Bursty**. Expand the **Description** attribute and edit the value of the **Ftp** attribute. Set the **Inter-Request Time (secs)** attribute to **exponential(0.1)**. Set the **File Size (bytes)** attribute to **constant(1000)**. In both cases, you will need to set the **Special Value** field to **Not Used** in order to modify the attribute values. The application you have now defined will transfer an average of ten 1-KB files every second. The exponential distribution is often used to model waiting times so we can use it here to model the time between file requests. Click on **OK** to close the window.

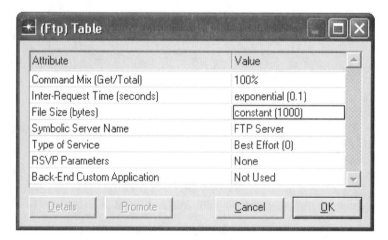

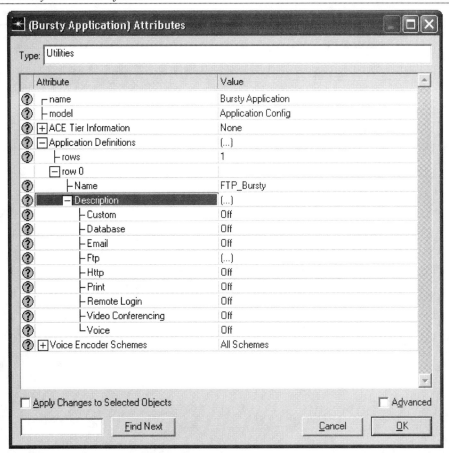

Select a **Profile Config** object from the Object Palette and place it in the project workspace. Right click on the object and choose **Edit Attributes**. Set the **name** attribute to **Bursty Profile**. Expand the **Profile Configuration** attribute and set the **rows** attribute to **1**. Expand the **row 0** attribute and set the **Profile Name** to **FTP_Bursty_Profile**. Expand the **Applications** attribute and set the **rows** attribute to **1**. Expand the **row 0** attribute and set the **Name** to **FTP_Bursty**. Set the **Repeatability** attribute to **Once at Start Time**. Click on **OK** to close the window.

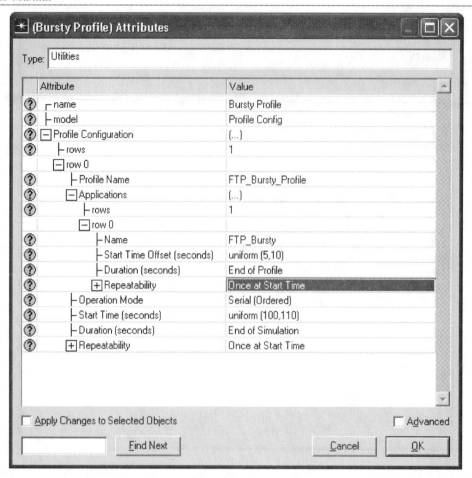

Select an **fr32_cloud** object from the Object Palette and place it in the project workspace. Right click on the cloud and choose **View Node Description**. The cloud represents a WAN that consists of Frame-Relay-capable switches and that supports up to 32 Frame Relay connections.

Right click on the cloud and select **Set Name**. Set the name to **Frame_Relay_Cloud**. Click on **OK** to close the window.

Select an **fr_wkstn_adv** device from the Object Palette and place it in the project workspace. Right click on the station and choose **View Node Description**. Note that the station supports the Frame Relay protocol. We will now set up the client to use the bursty FTP application that we defined.

Right click on the station and choose **Edit Attributes**. Modify the **name** attribute of the device to **Bursty Client**. Edit the **Application: Supported Profiles** attribute. Insert a row and set the **Profile Name** to **FTP_Bursty_Profile**. Click on **OK** to close the window.

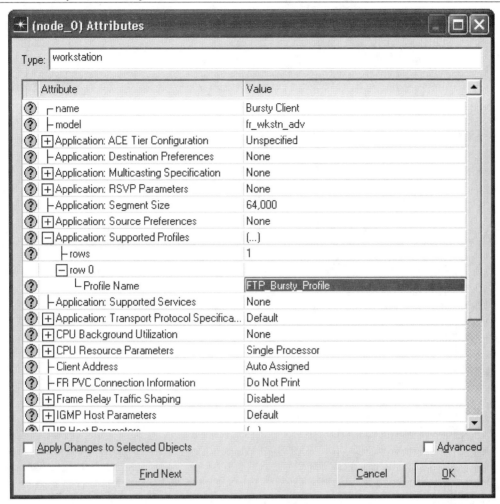

Select an **fr_server_adv** device from the Object Palette and place it in the project workspace.   Right click on the server and choose **View Node Description**.   Note that the server also supports the Frame Relay protocol. We will now set up the server to support the Bursty FTP application that we defined.

Right click on the device and choose **Edit Attributes**. Modify the **name** attribute of the server to **Bursty Server**. Edit the **Application: Supported Services** attribute. Insert a row and set the **Name** to **FTP_Bursty**. Click on **OK** to close the table window. Click on **OK** to close the window.

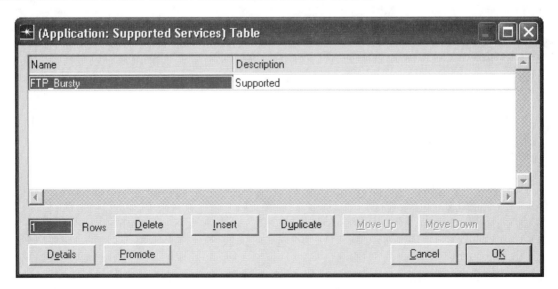

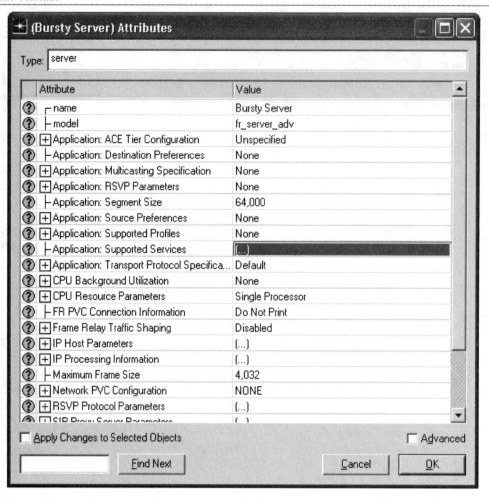

Select two **fr8_switch_adv** objects from the Object Palette. Place one next to the client and one next to the server. Right click on one of the switches and choose **View Node Description**. Note that the switch takes action when it becomes congested. It will discard the frames marked with the Discard Eligible Bit first, but may even discard normal frames. Click on the close window icon to close the window.

Right click on the client's switch and select **Set Name**. Set the name to **Client Switch**. Click on **OK** to close the window.

Right click on the server's switch and select **Set Name**. Set the name to **Server Switch**. Click on **OK** to close the window.

Select three **FR_T1_int** links from the Object Palette, and use them to connect the client to its switch, the server to its switch and the two switches to the Frame Relay cloud. Remember that T1 speed is 1.5 Mbps.

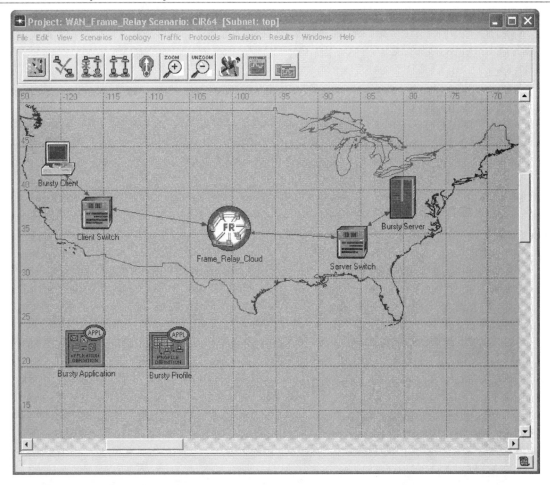

Finally, we can set up a permanent virtual circuit (PVC) between the client and the server so that they can communicate. Select an **FR PVC Config** object from the Object Palette, and place it in the project workspace. Right click on it and select **Set Name**. Set the **Name** to **PVC Config.** The **FR PVC Config** object must be placed in the workspace before any PVCs may be set up. Click on **OK** to close the window.

Select an **fr_pvc** object from the Object Palette and use it to connect the client to the server. When you right click to finish placing the PVC, choose **Abort Demand Definition**.

Right click on the PVC, and expand the **Contract Parameters** attribute. These parameters constitute the agreement between the end systems (client and server) and the Frame Relay service provider. Set the **Outgoing CIR (bits/sec)** attribute to **64000**. Set the **Outgoing Bc (bits)** to **64000**. Set the **Outgoing Be (bits)** to **32000**. The Committed Information Rate (CIR) is the amount of traffic that the service provider has agreed to carry. The committed burst size (Bc) indicates how much data can be sent in a given interval. In this case, the interval is one second, so the CIR = Bc. The excess burst size (Be) is the amount of traffic that the service provider may accept in addition to the committed rate, if network conditions allow. Excess data may be discarded if the service provider's network becomes congested. Click on **OK** to close the window.

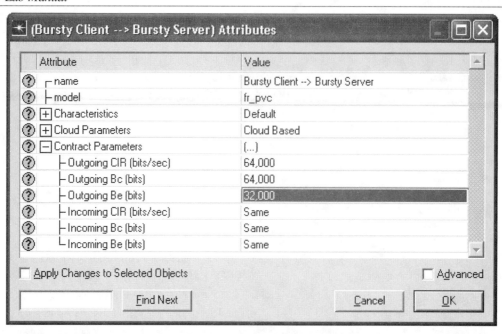

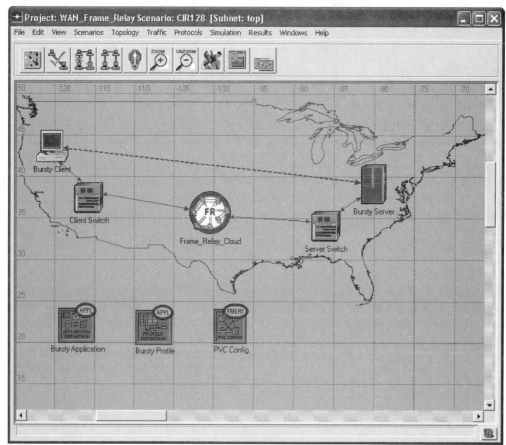

Configure and Run the Simulation

Select the **Simulation** tab => **Choose Individual Statistics...**
Expand the **Global Statistics** item and the **Frame Relay** item, and select the **Delay (sec), Delay Variance**, and **Residual Error Rate** statistics.
Expand the **FTP** item, and select the **Download Response Time (sec)** and **Traffic Received (bytes/sec)** statistics.

Expand the **Node Statistics** item and the **Frame Relay PVC** item, and select the **BECN Status, DE Status,** and **FECN Status** statistics.
Click on **OK** to close the window.

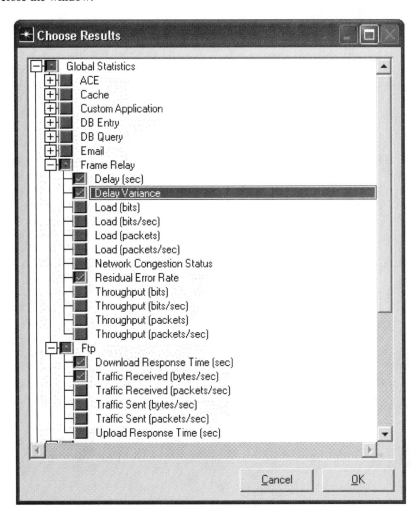

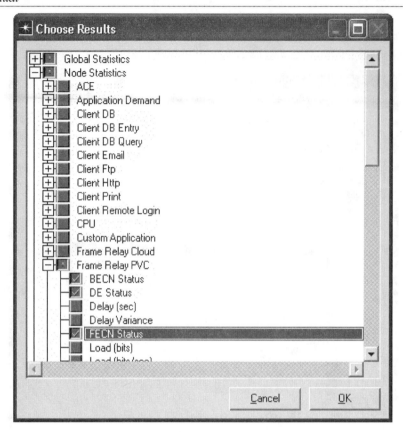

Select **Simulation => Configure Discrete Event Simulation...**
Under the **Common** tab, set the **Duration** to **5** and the unit to **minute(s)**.
Click on **OK** to close the window.

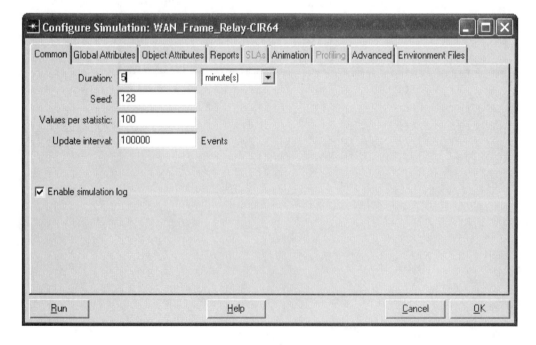

Duplicate the Scenario

We are now going to duplicate the scenario and configure the PVC to support a higher data rate. This will allow us to compare the performance across the two PVC rates. Choose **Scenarios => Duplicate Scenario**, and name the new scenario **CIR128**.

Right click on the PVC, and expand the **Contract Parameters** attribute. Set the **Outgoing CIR (bits/sec)** attribute to **128000**. Set the **Outgoing Bc (bits)** to **128000**. Leave the **Outgoing Be (bits)** unchanged at **32000**. Click on **OK** to close the window.

Run the Simulation

Select the **Scenarios** tab => **Manage Scenarios...**
Edit the **Results** field in both rows and set the value to **<collect>** or **<recollect>**.
Click on **OK** to run both scenarios (one after the other).
When the simulation has completed, click on **Close** to close window.

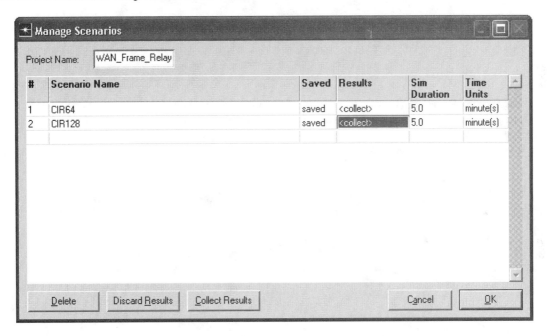

Inspect and Analyze Results

Select the **Results** tab => **Compare Results...**

Select and expand the **Global Statistics** item and the **Ftp** item, and select the **Download Response Time (sec)** statistic. Use **As Is** mode to view this statistic. Click on **Show** to see a more detailed graph. The statistic shows how long each download took, and there will be one point for each file downloaded. You can see that the downloads took much less time in the CIR128 case and that the variation in download times was much less. This is to be expected since there was more capacity available to the application in the second scenario. Click on the close window icon and choose to **Delete** the panel. Click on the statistic again to disable the preview.

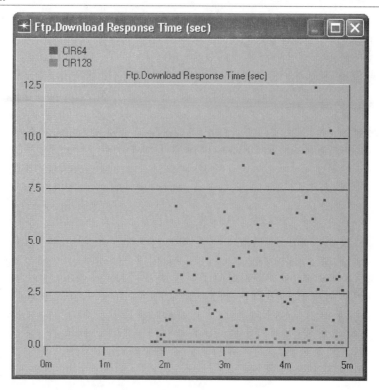

Expand the **Traffic Received (bytes/sec)** statistic and view using **As Is** mode. Click on **Show** to see a more detailed graph. This statistic shows the total amount of FTP traffic received by both the server and client. You can see that more traffic is received in the CIR128 case, and that there is more variation than in the CIR64 case. Click on the close window icon and choose to **Delete** the panel. Click on the statistic again to disable the preview.

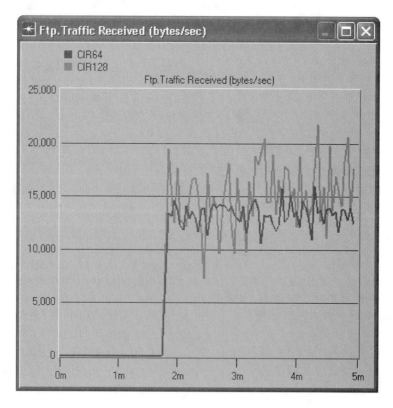

Select and expand the **Global Statistics** item and the **Frame Relay** item, and select the **Delay (sec)** statistic. Use **time_average** mode to view this statistic as this mode will make it easier to see the difference in performance. Click on the **Show** button to see more detail. The statistic shows how long each frame took to be delivered. You can see that the delay is greater in the CIR64 case and that the delay is growing over time. This is due to longer delays within the switches due to full buffers. Click on the close window icon and **Delete** the panel. Click on the statistic again to disable the preview.

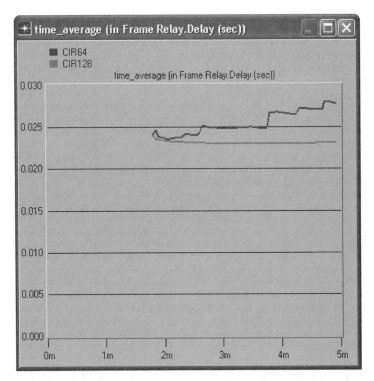

Expand the **Delay Variance (sec)** statistic and view using **As Is** mode. Click on **Show**. This statistic shows the variance in frame delivery delay. The CIR64 case shows much more variability and the variability is growing over time. Click on the close window icon and **Delete** the panel. Click on the statistic again to disable the preview.

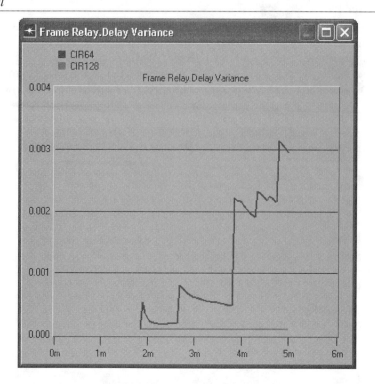

Expand the **Residual Error Rate** statistic and view using **As Is** mode. Click on **Show**. This statistic shows the percentage of frames which are discarded due to congestion or corruption. You can see that many more frames are discarded in the CIR64 case and that the percentage is growing as the switch becomes more and more congested. Click on the close window icon and **Delete** the panel. Click on the statistic again to disable the preview.

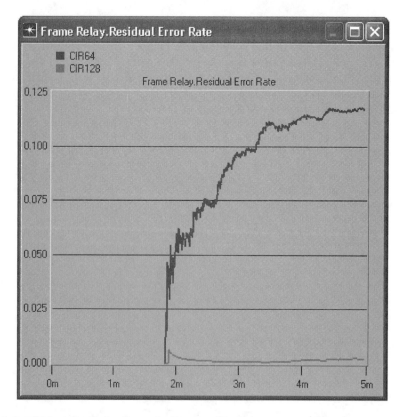

Select and expand the **Object Statistics** item, the **Bursty Client** item, and the **Frame Relay PVC** item. Select the **DE Status** statistic and view using **As Is** mode. Click on **Show**. This statistic shows the number of frames which were received by the client which had the DE bit set. When many frames are received with the DE bit set, that indicates that the source of the frames was frequently sending faster than the contracted CIR. You can see that far more frames are marked with the DE bit in the CIR64 case. This makes sense since the application produces the same amount of traffic in both scenarios, but the CIR128 scenario provides more capacity for carrying the traffic. Click on the close window icon and **Delete** the panel. Click on the statistic again to disable the preview.

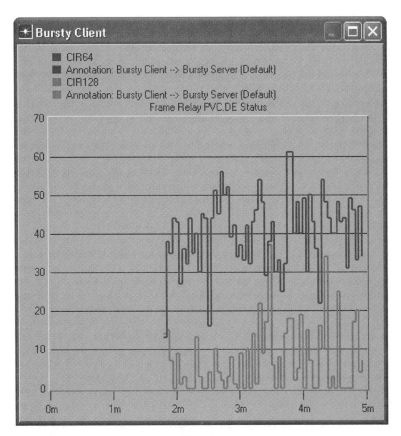

The **BECN Status** or **FECN Status** statistics show how many frames were received with the BECN or FECN bits set. These bits are set by the switch when it is congested. If you view these statistics, you will see that no frames were received with the bits set. The offered traffic is not sufficient yet to cause congestion at the switches.

Save your model and close all windows.

Questions

1. How much traffic is being generated by the Bursty Server? You can calculate this data rate using the **Inter-Request Time** and **File Size** parameters you set when configuring the bursty application.

2. Given the traffic level calculated in Question 1, explain how this traffic can be carried given the speed of the links used to connect the devices, and the contract parameters of the PVC connecting the client and server.

3. Duplicate the CIR64 scenario, and replace the T1 link between the client and its switch with an **FR_DS0_int** link. Remember that DS0 speed is 64 Kbps. Rerun the simulation and inspect the **BECN Status** and **FECN Status** statistics for both the **Bursty Client** and **Bursty Server**. How do they compare to the CIR64 scenario results? Explain your results. Explain the usage of the BECN and FECN bits in the Frame Relay header. Also inspect the **Residual Error Rate** statistic. How does it compare to the CIR64 case?

4. Frame Relay service providers often offer Frame Relay PVC contracts called *zero CIR*. In these cases, *all* packets are marked discard eligible. Zero CIR service is usually less expensive, but provides fewer guarantees.

Duplicate the CIR64 scenario, and edit the PVC attributes. Set all the **Contract Parameters** to zero. Rerun the simulation and compare your results to the CIR64 results. What differences did you find? What would be the effect on the Traffic Received at the Bursty Client if you added another client with a CIR of 64 Kbps to the zero CIR case? Explain your answer.

5. In Question 3, some frames are discarded due to congestion at the switch. The congestion can be relieved if the traffic source transmits frames less frequently. Frame Relay systems provide traffic shaping algorithms to restrain the traffic source from sending too quickly. Duplicate the DS0 scenario from Question 3, and edit the Bursty Server attributes. Expand the **Frame Relay Traffic Shaping** attribute, and set the **Status** to **Enabled**. Click on the question mark to the left of each of the traffic shaping attributes to determine their function. Calculate values for these attributes that will result in an uncongested network; in other words, restrict the data rate to less than the speed of the DS0 line (64 Kbps). Write down the function of each attribute, the value you calculated, and an explanation of the calculations. Run the simulation and gather statistics to show that you achieved the goal of reducing congestion (and corresponding frame discards).

Lab 5   Quality of Service: Impact of Queuing Policy

Overview

In a store-and-forward network, routers maintain one or more queues for each output line. These are necessary as a packet may arrive and be destined for a line which is already busy. A queuing policy defines a set of rules for placing packets into the queue and taking them back out. The traditional policy is First-In, First-Out (FIFO), which is easy to implement and treats all data streams the same. A packet which has newly arrived is placed at the end of the queue and waits its turn to be sent.

Now that the Internet is also used to carry voice and video streams, simple FIFO mechanisms are not sufficient. Voice and video applications require bounds on the delay and delay variation (jitter) that a packet will experience. One way to implement these bounds is to treat the packets differently within the router's queues. In the Weighted Fair Queuing (WFQ) policy, one queue is maintained for each priority class. Weights are associated with the classes based on their importance. Queues are then serviced (i.e., packets are taken from the queues and sent on the outgoing line) at rates based on their weights. For instance, if queue A was assigned a weight of one, and queue B was assigned a weight of two, then two packets would be sent from queue B for every one sent from queue A. By assigning voice and video streams to a queue with higher weight, they can be given precedence over standard data traffic.

In the Priority Queuing policy, multiple queues are again maintained based on the priority classes assigned to the packets. In this case though, *all* high-priority packets get sent before any low-priority packets. If we have two queues, one configured to handle priority-one traffic, and one configured to handle priority-two traffic, the priority-two queue will be serviced until it is empty, and only then will the priority-one queue be serviced. Priority one transmissions will be preempted if any new priority-two packets arrive.

Objective

To examine the effects of applying different router queuing policies. We will examine packet loss rate due to buffer overflow at the router, queuing delay, and queuing delay variation.

Build the Simulation Model

Start up OPNET IT Guru Academic Edition.
Select the **File** tab => **New...**
Choose **Project** and click on **OK**.
Change the **Project Name** to **xx_QOS_Queuing** (where **xx** are your initials). Set the **Scenario Name** to **PQ** and click on **OK**.
In the **Initial Topology** window, select **Create Empty Scenario** and click on **Next**.
In the **Choose Network Scale** window, select **Choose from Maps** and click on **Next**.
In the **Choose Map** window, choose **usa** and click on **Next**.
In the **Select Technologies** window, click on **Next**.
In the **Review** window, click on **OK**.

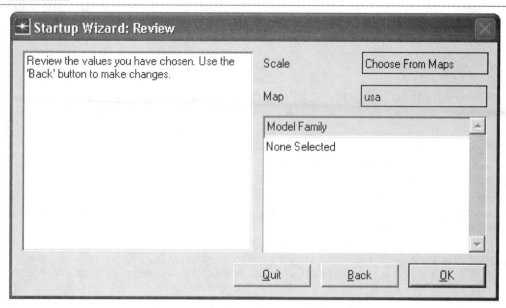

First, we will configure two FTP-based applications which are identical, except for the priorities associated with them.

Select an **Application Config** object from the Object Palette and place it in the project workspace. Right click on the object and choose **Edit Attributes**. Set the **name** attribute to **Applications**.

Expand the **Application Definitions** attribute and set the **rows** attribute to **2**. Expand the **row 0** attribute and set the **Name** attribute to **FTP_Low_Priority_Application**. Expand the **Description** attribute and edit the value of the **Ftp** attribute. Set the **Inter-Request Time (secs)** attribute to **exponential(5)**. Set the **File Size (bytes)** attribute to **constant(500000)**. In both cases, you will need to set the **Special Value** field to **Not Used** in order to modify the attribute values. Notice that the **Type of Service** field is set to **Best Effort (0)**. Best Effort is the lowest priority level. The application you have now defined will transfer one 500 KB file after another with an average of 5 seconds between the transfers. Click on **OK** to close the window.

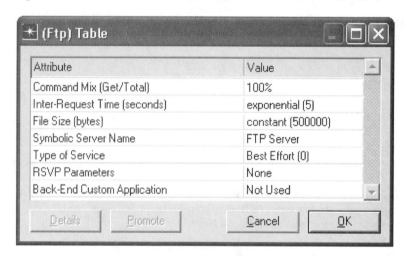

Now expand the **row 1** attribute and set the name to **FTP_High_Priority_Application**. Again, set the **Inter-Request Time (secs)** to **exponential(5)** and the **File Size (bytes)** to **constant(500000)**. Next, change the **Type of Service** field to **Excellent Effort (3)**. Excellent Effort provides a higher priority than Best Effort.
Click on **OK** twice to close the windows.

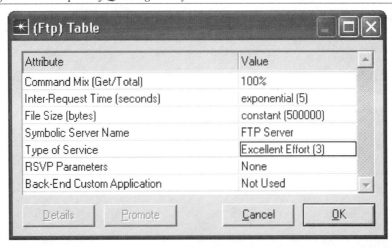

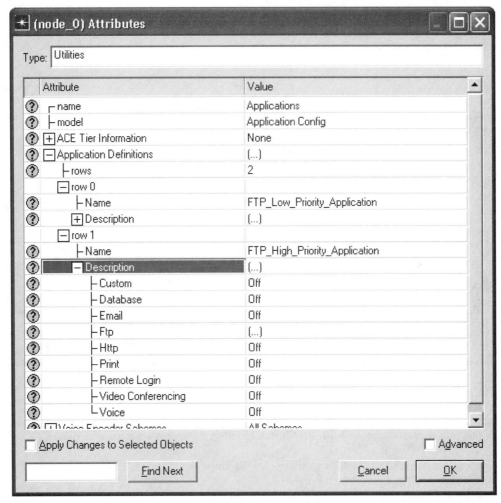

Select a **Profile Config** object from the Object Palette and place it in the project workspace. Right click on the object and choose **Edit Attributes**. Set the **name** attribute to **Profiles**.

Expand the **Profile Configuration** attribute and set the **rows** attribute to **2**. Expand the **row 0** attribute and set the **Profile Name** to **FTP_Low_Priority_Profile**. Expand the **Applications** attribute and set the **rows** attribute to **1**. Expand the **row 0** attribute and set the **Name** to **FTP_Low_Priority_Application**. Set the **Duration (seconds)** to **End of Last Task**. Expand the **Repeatability** attribute and set the **Inter-repetition Time (seconds)** to **constant(0)**.

Expand the **row 1** attribute, and set the **Profile Name** to **FTP_High_Priority_Profile**. Expand the **Applications** attribute and set the **rows** attribute to **1**. Expand the **row 0** attribute and set the **Name** to

FTP_High_Priority_Application. Set the **Duration (seconds)** to **End of Last Task**. Expand the **Repeatability** attribute and set the **Inter-repetition Time (seconds)** to **constant(0)**.
Click on **OK** to close the window.

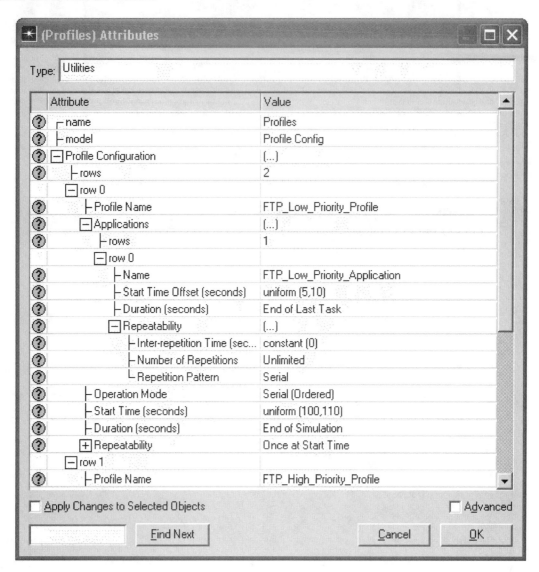

Now that we have profiles created, we will build a network to use them.

Select a **ppp_wkstn** device from the Object Palette and place it in the project workspace.
Right click on the station and choose **Edit Attributes**. Modify the **name** attribute of the device to **FTP Low Client**.
Edit the **Application: Supported Profiles** attribute. Set the **rows** attribute to **1**, expand the **row 0** attribute, and set the **Profile Name** to **FTP_Low_Priority_Profile**.
Click on **OK** to close the window.

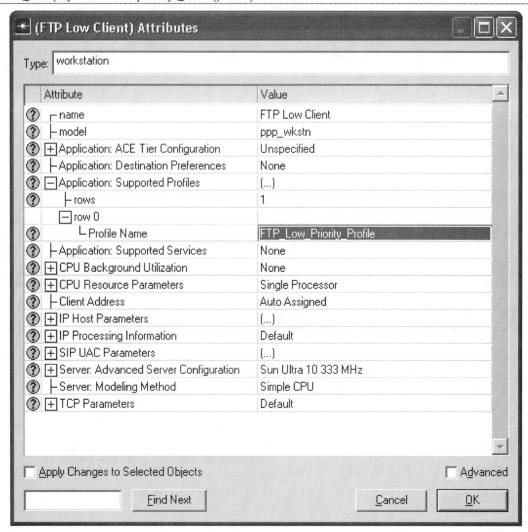

Select another **ppp_wkstn** device from the Object Palette and place it in the project workspace.
Right click on the station and choose **Edit Attributes**. Modify the **name** attribute of the device to **FTP High Client**.
Edit the **Application: Supported Profiles** attribute. Set the **rows** attribute to **1**, expand the **row 0** attribute, and set the **Profile Name** to **FTP_High_Priority_Profile**.
Click on **OK** to close the window.

Select a **ppp_server** device from the Object Palette and place it in the project workspace.
We will now set up the server to support both FTP applications that we defined.
Right click on the device and choose **Edit Attributes**. Modify the **name** attribute of the server to **FTP Server**.
Edit the **Application: Supported Services** attribute. Set the **rows** attribute to **2**.   Set the **Name** in the first row to **FTP_Low_Priority_Application**. Set the **Name** in the second row to **FTP_High_Priority_Application**.
Click on **OK** twice to close the windows.

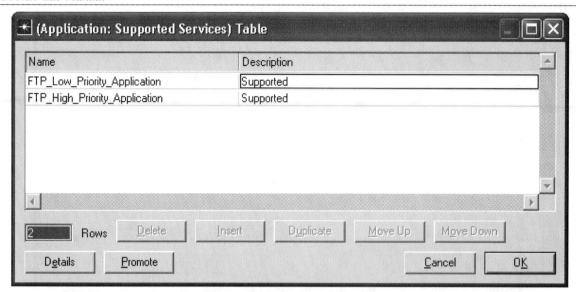

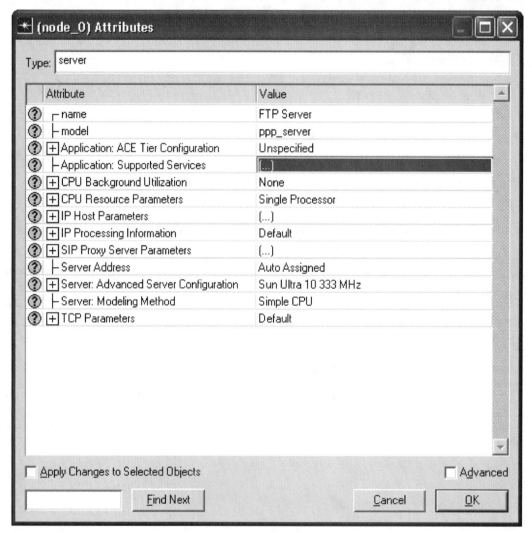

Select 2 **ethernet4_slip8_gtwy** devices from the Object Palette and place them in the project workspace. Right click on the first router and choose **Set Name**. Set the **Name** to **Router 1**. Right click on the second router and choose **Set Name**. Set the **Name** to **QoS Router**.

Select **PPP_DS1** links from the Object Palette and use them to connect the two FTP clients to Router 1, and to connect the two routers together. Select a **PPP_DS3** link from the Object Palette and use it to connect the FTP Server to the QoS Router.

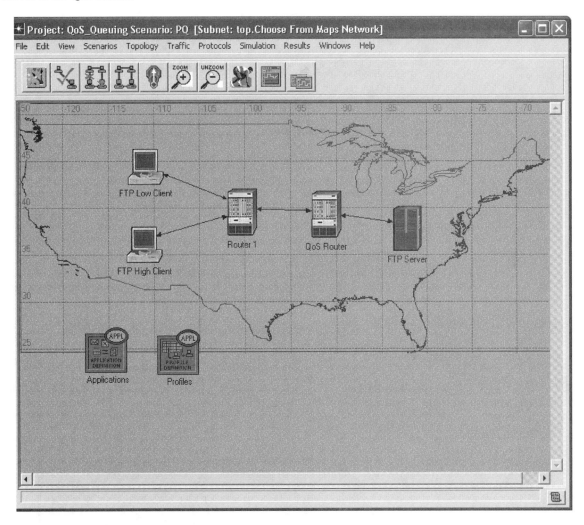

Then we need to set up the queuing mechanisms to be used by the routers.

Right click on the QoS Router and choose **Select Similar Nodes** so that we can apply changes to both routers at the same time. Select the **Protocols** tab => **IP** => **QoS** => **Configure QoS...** Set the **QoS** Scheme to **Priority Queuing**. Note that the **QoS profile** is **ToS Based**, which means that the router will use the Type of Service field in the IP packet header to determine which packets get priority. The Best Effort and Excellent Effort priorities that we defined earlier are represented using the ToS field.
Click on the radio button next to **Interfaces on selected router(s)**.
Click on **OK** to close the window.

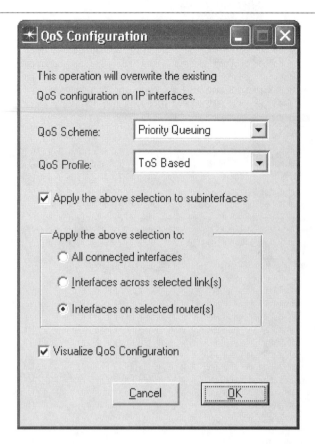

You have now configured the QoS Router to use the priority queuing mechanism on its interfaces. Note that a **QoS Config** object automatically appears in the project workspace. This is due to the fact that we configured the QoS Router to use queuing mechanisms.

Right click on the PPP link that connects the QoS Router and Router 1, and choose **Edit Attributes**. Inspect the **port a** and **port b** attributes to see which interface is being used on the QoS Router (IF10 in our example). Your configuration may differ from the one shown, depending on how you placed your PPP link. Click on **OK** to close the window.

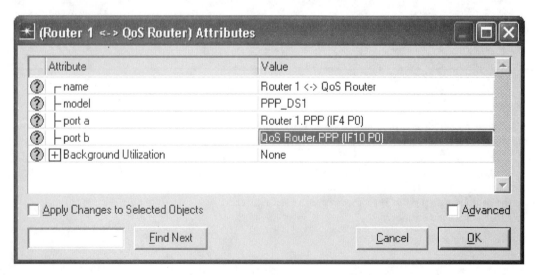

Right click on the QoS Router and choose **Edit Attributes**. Expand the **IP Routing Parameters** item, the **Interface Information** item, and the row item for the interface you just found, **row 10** in our example. Expand the **QoS Information** item. Edit the **Buffer Size (bytes)** attribute and set the value to **100000**. By making the buffer size on this interface relatively small, buffer overflow will occur more quickly, allowing us to see the results of the different queuing mechanisms more easily. Note that overflow would eventually occur anyway since the FTP Server is generating lots of traffic over the DS3 line which connects it to the QoS Router, but the QoS Router has only a DS1 line to forward traffic on to the clients.

Click on **OK** to close the window.

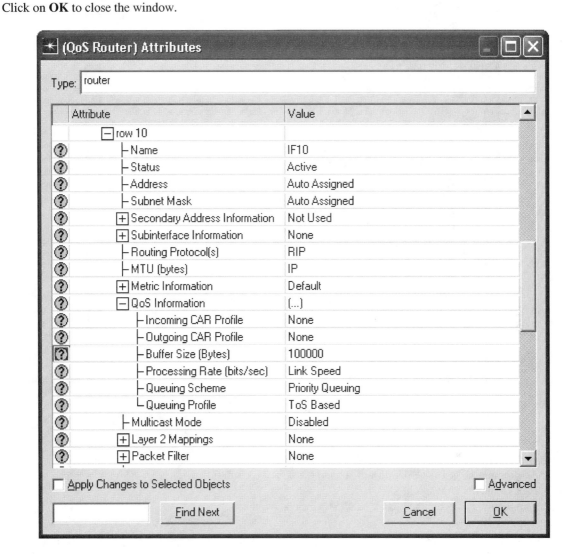

Configure and Run the Simulation

Right click on the QoS Router and select **Choose Individual Statistics**. Expand the **IP Interface** item, and select the **Buffer Usage (packets)**, the **Queue Delay Variation (sec)**, the **Queuing Delay (sec)**, and the **Traffic Dropped (packets/sec)** statistics. Click on **OK** to close the window.

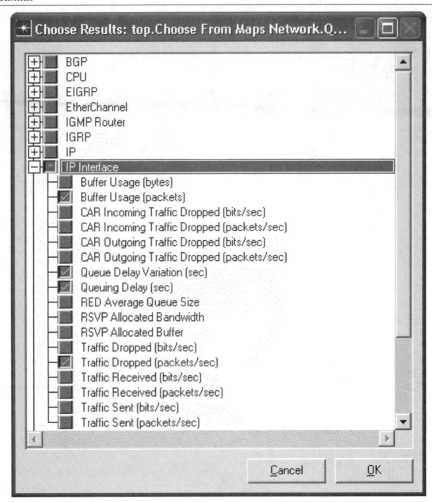

Select **Simulation => Configure Discrete Event Simulation...**
Under the **Common** tab, set the **Duration** to **10**, and the unit to **minute(s)**.
Click on **Run** to run the simulation.
When the simulation has completed, click on **Close** to close window.

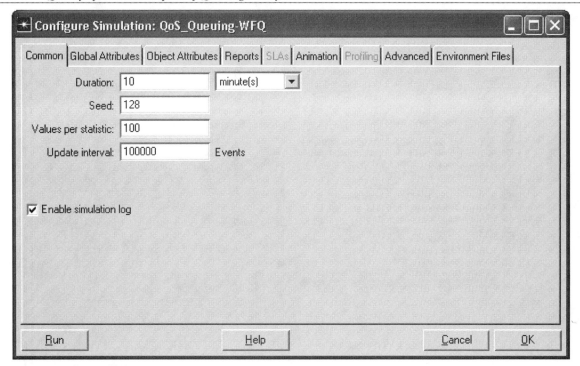

Inspect and Analyze Results

Select the **Results** tab => **View Results...**

Select and expand the **Object Statistics** item, the **Choose From Maps Network** item, the **QoS Router** item, and the **IP Interface** item.   Select the **PQ Traffic Dropped (packets/sec) IF10 Q1** and **PQ Traffic Dropped (packets/sec) IF10 Q0 (Default Queue)** statistics.   Note that interface 10 (IF10) is the interface on the QoS router which connects it to Router 1. If, during configuration setup, you found that a different interface was used in your model, replace IF10 with that interface for the rest of the results analysis steps. Use the **As Is** mode to view all statistics. The selected statistics show how many packets were dropped due to buffer overflow. Q1 corresponds to the high-priority traffic and Q0 corresponds to the low-priority traffic. Note that the high-priority queue has a lower drop rate than the low-priority queue. Click on the statistics again to disable the preview.

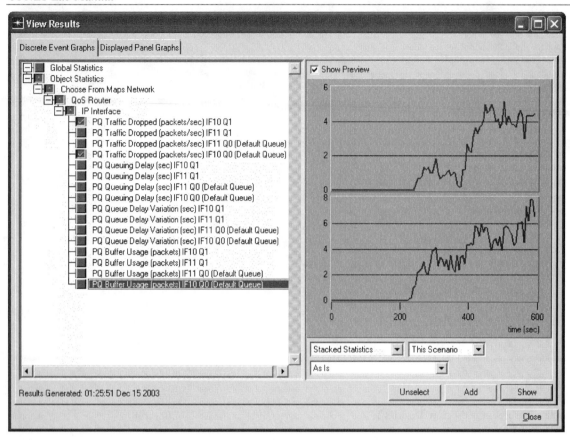

Select the **PQ Queuing Delay (sec) IF10 Q1** and **PQ Queuing Delay (sec) IF10 Q0 (Default Queue)** statistics. These statistics show how long packets had to wait in the queue before being sent. You can see that the low-priority traffic (Q0) experienced drastically longer queuing delay than the high-priority traffic (Q1). Click on the statistics again to disable the preview.

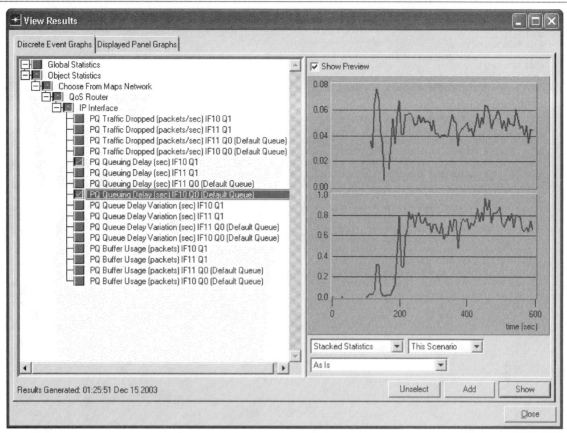

Select the **PQ Queue Delay Variation (sec) IF10 Q1** and **PQ Queue Delay Variation (sec) IF10 Q0 (Default Queue)** statistics.   These statistics show the *variation* in queuing delay (jitter) that packets experienced. Again, the high-priority traffic experiences much less jitter than the low-priority traffic. Click on the statistics again to disable the preview.

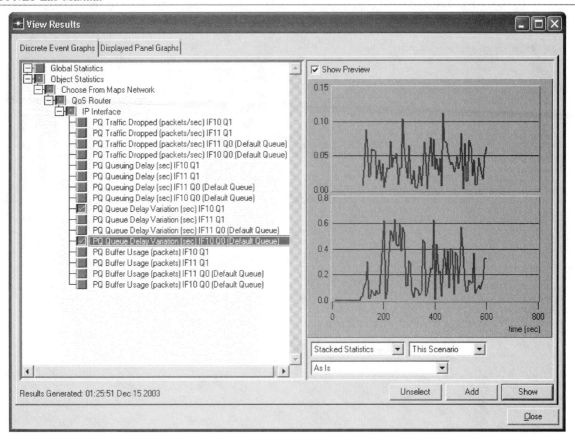

Select the **PQ Buffer Usage (packets) IF10 Q1** and **PQ Buffer Usage (packets) IF10 Q0 (Default Queue)** statistics. These statistics show how many packets were waiting in the queue at any time during the simulation. You can see that many low-priority packets were waiting in the queue at all times, while high-priority packets were seldom kept waiting. Click on the statistics again to disable the preview.

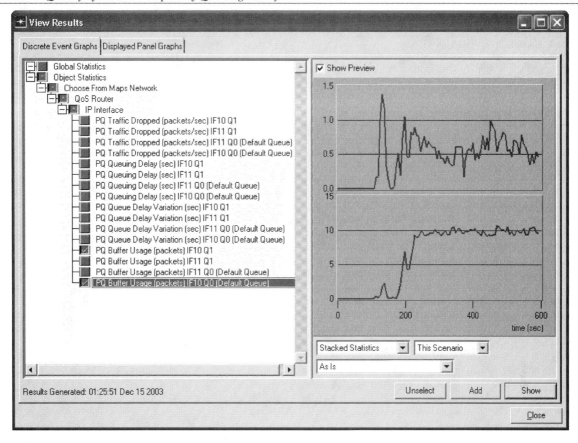

Save your model and close all windows.

Questions

1. Duplicate your scenario and name it **WFQ** (for Weighted Fair Queuing). Select both routers and choose the **Protocols** tab => **IP** => **QoS** => **Configure QoS…** Set the **QoS** Scheme to **WFQ**. Note that the **QoS profile** is **ToS Based**, which means that the router will use the ToS field that we defined for the application to determine which packets get priority.
Click on the radio button next to **Interfaces on selected router(s)**.
Click on **OK** to close the window.
Rerun the simulation and examine the relative packet drop rate, delay, delay variation, and buffer occupancy. Explain your results.

2. Duplicate your scenario and name it **FIFO**. Select the two routers and choose the **Protocols** tab => **IP** => **QoS** => **Configure QoS…** Set the **QoS** Scheme to **FIFO**. FIFO routers treat all packets the same. No priorities are implemented.
Click on the radio button next to **Interfaces on selected router(s)**.
Click on **OK** to close the window.
Rerun the simulation and examine the relative packet drop rate, delay, delay variation, and buffer occupancy. Explain your results.

3. Compare the Weighted Fair Queuing, Priority Queuing, and FIFO schemes in terms of drop rate, delay, and delay variation. What are the advantages and disadvantages of each?

4. Edit the attributes of the QoS Parameters object. Look in the WFQ Profiles attribute at the ToS based profile. What weights are associated with the various ToS values in the WFQ scheme? How do these weights affect the operation of the router?

5. Edit the attributes of the QoS Parameters object. Look in the Priority Queuing Profiles at the ToS based profile. How many priority levels are defined? What ToS values are associated with each priority level?

6. Edit the attributes of the QoS Parameters object. Look in both the Priority Queuing Profiles and the WFQ Profiles. Other than ToS, how else may packets be classified for priority service?

Lab 6   Quality of Service: Impact of Traffic Shaping

Overview

The shape of the traffic that is offered to a network can have a large effect on the resulting delay and variation in delay that the traffic experiences. Smooth, regular traffic patterns are generally easier for routers to handle than bursty, irregular patterns. When a large burst of traffic arrives, a router may not have sufficient capacity to immediately forward the packets, and it must place the packets in a queue. The packets will wait there until capacity is available. In the meantime, the packets experience increased delay. If the size of the queue varies over time (due again to irregular traffic patterns), incoming packets will experience different amounts of queuing delay. In general, for any application, it is desirable to reduce delay. Applications based on voice and video, however, cannot tolerate a large amount of delay variation either.

Traffic-shaping schemes, such as leaky bucket or token bucket, are designed to smooth out the traffic patterns at the source. The hope is that smoother patterns will see less delay and less variation in delay.

Objective

To examine the effects of traffic shaping on router performance. We will examine buffer usage, queuing delay, and queuing delay variation when generating constant bit rate (CBR) traffic, and two varieties of bursty traffic.

Build the Simulation Model

Start up OPNET IT Guru Academic Edition.
Select the **File** tab => **New...**
Choose **Project** and click on **OK**.
Change the **Project Name** to **xx_QoS_Shaping** (where **xx** are your initials). Set the **Scenario Name** to **CBR** and click on **OK**.
In the **Initial Topology** window, select **Create Empty Scenario** and click on **Next**.
In the **Choose Network Scale** window, select **Office** and click on **Next**.
In the **Specify Size** window, click on **Next**.
In the **Select Technologies** window, click on **Next**.
In the **Review** window, click on **OK**.

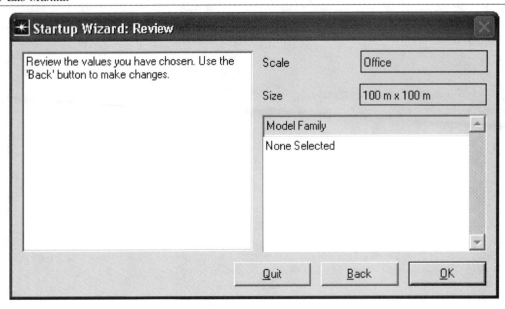

First, we will modify the existing **File Print (Heavy)** application to generate traffic at a constant bit rate. The File Print application is based on a simple model and is easy to modify.

Select an **Application Config** object from the Object Palette and place it in the project workspace. Right click on the object and choose **Edit Attributes**. Set the **name** attribute to **Applications**.

Edit the **Application Definitions** attribute and set the value to **Default**. Now expand the **Application Definitions** item, the **row 6** item (which corresponds to the **File Print (Heavy)** application) and the **Description** item. Edit the **Print** attribute. Set the **Print Interarrival Time (seconds)** attribute to **constant(0.0055)**. Set the **File Size (bytes)** attribute to **constant(1000)**. The application you have now defined will transfer one 1000 byte file every 0.0055 second (5.5 milliseconds) without variation. Click on **OK** to close the window.

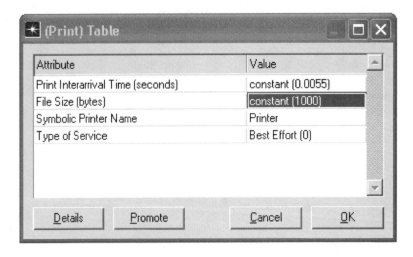

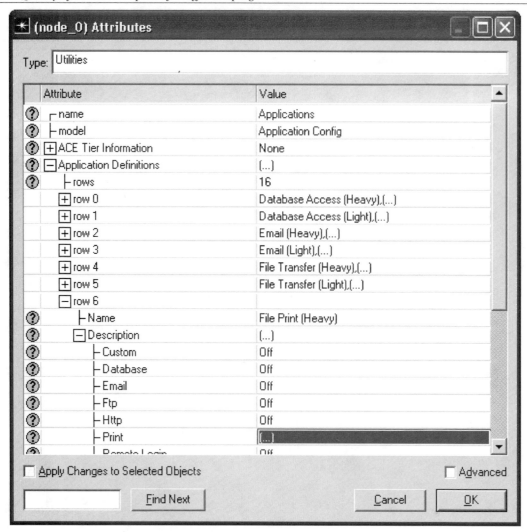

Select a **Profile Config** object from the Object Palette and place it in the project workspace. Right click on the object and choose **Edit Attributes**. Set the **name** attribute to **Profiles**.

Expand the **Profile Configuration** attribute and set the **rows** attribute to **1**. Expand the **row 0** attribute and set the **Profile Name** to **Data Stream**. Expand the **Applications** attribute and set the **rows** attribute to **1**. Expand the **row 0** attribute and set the **Name** to **File Print (Heavy)**. Click on **OK** to close the window.

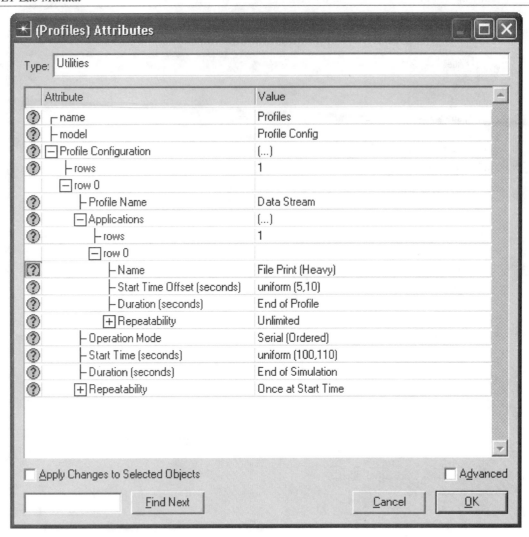

Select a **QoS Attribute Config** object from the Object Palette and place it in the project workspace. Right click on the object, choose **Set Name**, and set the **Name** to QoS. Click on **OK** to close the window. The QoS object is necessary as we will be configuring a router to do quality of service monitoring.

Now we will build a client-server system based on the file printing application and profile that we just created.

Click on **Configure Palette** in the Object Palette. Click on **Node Models**. Scroll down and choose to include the **ppp_server_adv** and **ppp_wkstn_adv** models. Click on **OK** twice, and choose to save your model to finish configuring the palette.

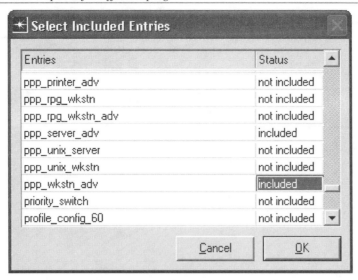

Select a **ppp_wkstn_adv** device from the Object Palette and place it in the project workspace.

Right click on the workstation and choose **Edit Attributes**. Modify the **name** attribute of the device to **Client**.

Edit the **Application: Supported Profiles** attribute. Set the **rows** attribute to **1**, expand the **row 0** attribute, and set the **Profile Name** to **Data Stream**. Expand the **Application: Transport Protocol Specification** attribute, and set the **Print Transport** attribute to **UDP**. Click on **OK** to close the window. By specifying that UDP be used rather than TCP, we eliminate the TCP connection setup and teardown overhead that would affect our results.

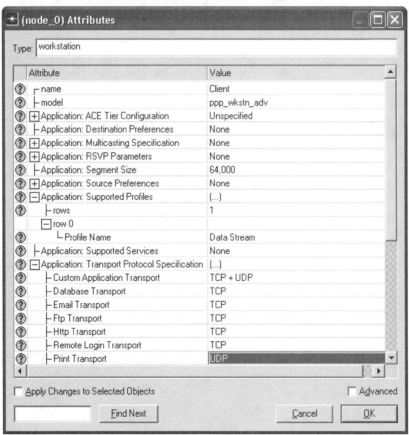

Select a **ppp_server_adv** device from the Object Palette and place in the project workspace. Right click on the device and choose **Edit Attributes**. Modify the **name** attribute of the server to **Server**.

Edit the **Application: Supported Services** attribute. Set the **rows** attribute to **1** and expand the **row 0** attribute. Set the **Name** to **File Print (Heavy)**. Click on **OK** to close the window. Expand the **Application: Transport Protocol Specification** attribute, and set the **Print Transport** attribute to **UDP**. Click on **OK** to close the window.

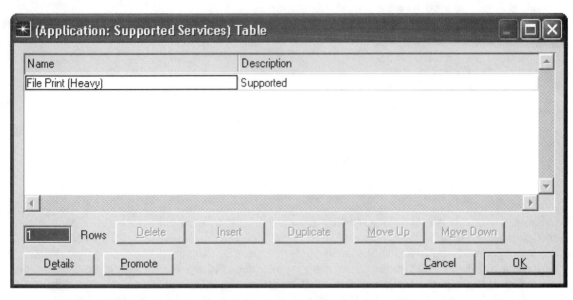

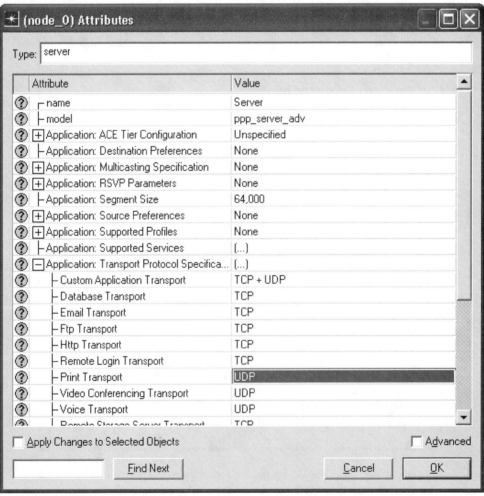

Select an **ethernet4_slip8_gtwy** device from the Object Palette and place it in the project workspace. Right click on the router and choose **Set Name**. Set the **Name** to **Router** and click on **OK** to close the window.

Select a **PPP_DS1** link from the Object Palette and use it to connect the server to the router. Select a **PPP_DS3** link from the Object Palette and use it to connect the client to the router. The inequality in data rates will help us to see the effects of different traffic-shaping schemes.

Right click on the PPP link which connects the Router and the Server, and choose **Edit Attributes**. Inspect the **port a** and **port b** attributes to see which interface is being used on the Router (IF10 in our example). Your configuration may differ from the one shown depending on how you placed your PPP link. You will need this interface information when viewing results. Click on **OK** to close the window.

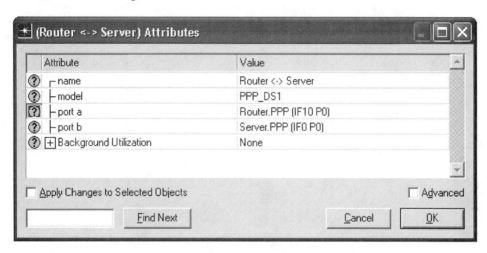

Left click on the router to select it, and then select the **Protocols** tab => **IP** => **QoS** => **Configure QoS…** Note that the default QoS scheme is FIFO (First-In First-Out). Click on the radio button marked **Interfaces on selected routers**, and click on **OK** to finish configuring quality of service on the router.

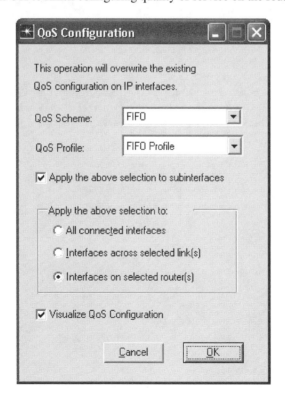

Our model is now complete.

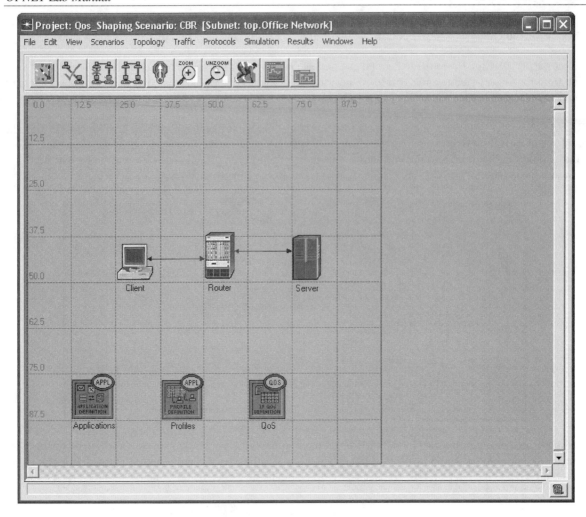

Configure the Simulation

Select the **Simulation** tab => **Choose Individual Statistics...** Expand the **Node Statistics** item and the **IP Interface** item, and select the **Buffer Usage (bytes)**, the **Queue Delay Variation (sec)**, the **Queuing Delay (sec)**, and the **Traffic Dropped (bits/sec)** statistics. Click on **OK** to close window.

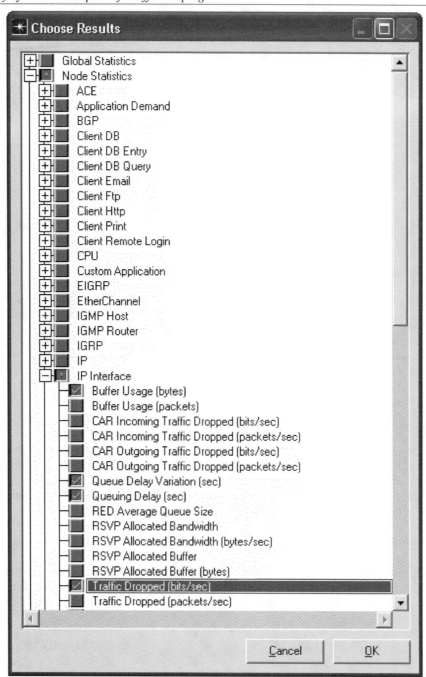

Select **Simulation => Configure Discrete Event Simulation...**
Under the **Common** tab, set the **Duration** to **250**, and the unit to **second(s)**.
Click on **OK** to close the window.

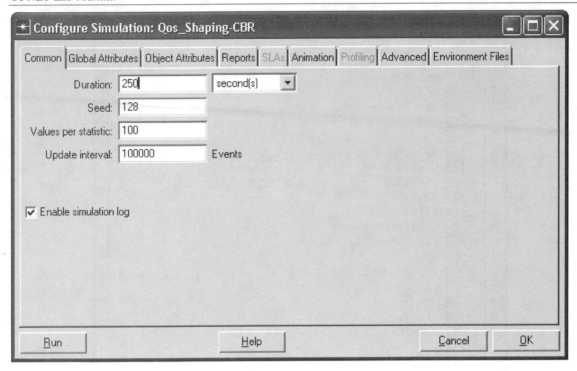

Duplicate the Scenario

We are now going to duplicate the scenario and change the characteristics of the data stream. We will create one scenario where the stream interarrivals are based on a uniform distribution, which provides somewhat variable interarrival times, and another based on the exponential distribution, which provides extremely variable interarrival times. In all three cases, however, the average amount of traffic generated per second will be the same. This will allow us to compare the effects on the router of traffic which is shaped differently.

Choose **Scenarios => Duplicate Scenario**, and name the new scenario **Uniform**. Click on **OK** to create the scenario.

Right click on the Applications node and choose **Edit Attributes**. Expand the **Application Definitions, row 6** (which corresponds to **File Print (Heavy)**), and **Description** attributes. Edit the **Print Interarrival Time (seconds)** attribute and set the value to **uniform(0.0005,0.0105)**. Click on **O K** twice to close the windows. Packets will now be generated at random intervals ranging from 0.5 to 10.5 milliseconds.

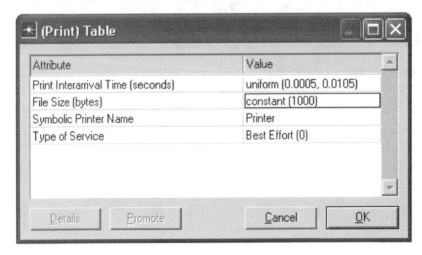

Choose **Scenarios** => **Duplicate Scenario**, and name the new scenario **Exponential**. Click on **OK** to create the scenario.

Right click on the Applications node and choose to **Edit Attributes**. Expand the **Application Definitions, row 6** (corresponding to **File Print (Heavy)**), and **Description** attributes. Edit the **Print Interarrival Time (seconds)** attribute and set the value to **exp(0.00055)**. Click on **OK** twice to close the windows. Packets will now be generated at random intervals with a mean of 5.5 milliseconds.

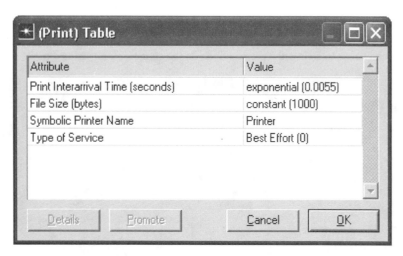

Run the Simulation

Select the **Scenarios** tab => **Manage Scenarios...**
Edit the **Results** field in all three rows and set the value to **<collect>** or **<recollect>**.
Click on **OK** to run the scenarios (one after the other).
When the simulation has completed, click on **Close** to close the window.

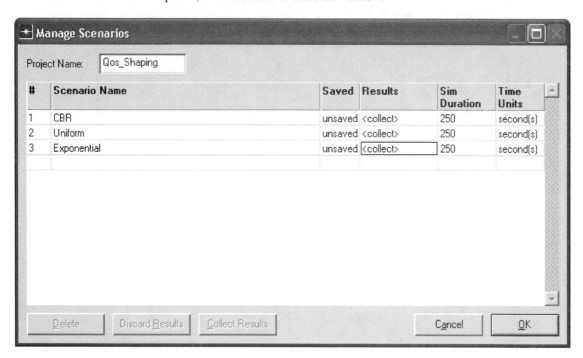

Inspect and Analyze Results

Select the **Results** tab => **Compare Results...**

Select and expand the **Object Statistics** item, the **Office Network** item, the **Router** item, and the **IP Interface** item. Select the **FIFO Buffer Usage (bytes) IF10 Q0** statistic. Note that interface 10 (IF10) is the interface on the Router that connects it to the Server. If, during configuration setup, you found that a different interface was used in your model, replace IF10 with that interface for the rest of the results analysis steps. Use the **As Is** mode to view all statistics. Click on **Show** to see a detailed version of the graph. This statistic shows how full the router's buffers were during the simulation. The buffers can fill up if a large burst of traffic is received at once. You can see that the router can handle the traffic easily if the packets are received at constant intervals. The buffer does not fill at all. When packets are received more irregularly, in the uniform distribution case, buffer usage begins to grow. When packets are received very irregularly, buffer usage is high. Click on the close window icon and choose to **Delete** the panel. Click on the statistic again to disable the preview.

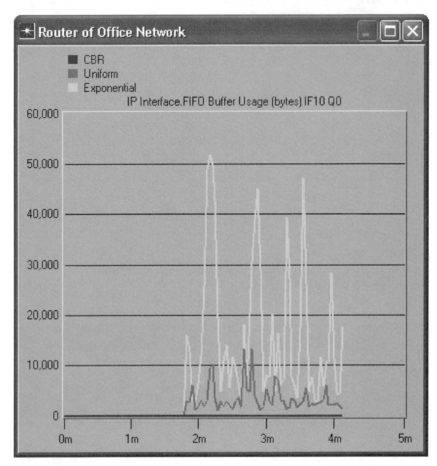

Select the **FIFO Queuing Delay (sec) IF10 Q0** statistic. Click on **Show** to see a detailed version of the graph. This statistic shows how long packets had to wait in the queue before being sent. As a router's buffers fill up, incoming packets must wait longer to be sent. Since the buffers were always empty in the CBR case, there is no queuing delay. The uniform case and exponential case see longer delays due to the high buffer usage in those cases. Click on the close window icon and choose to **Delete** the panel. Click on the statistic again to disable the preview.

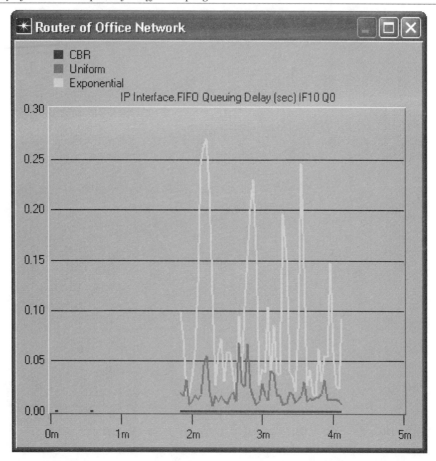

Select the **FIFO Queue Delay Variation (sec) IF10 Q0** statistic. Click on **Show** to see a detailed version of the graph. This statistic shows the variation in how long packets had to wait in the queue before being sent. When the size of the router's queue changes over time, the delay that each incoming packet sees will be different. The buffers were always empty in the CBR case, so the variation in queuing delay is zero. The uniform case and exponential case had buffers that filled and emptied often, causing a significant in variation delay. Click on the close window icon and choose to **Delete** the panel. Click on the statistic again to disable the preview.

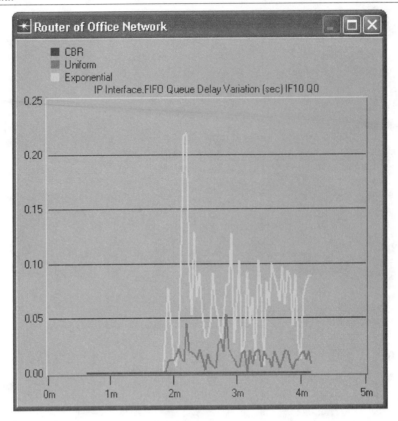

You may also inspect the **FIFO Traffic Dropped (bits/sec) IF10 Q0** statistic to see that no packets were dropped due to full buffers in any of the three scenarios.

Save your model and close all windows.

Questions

1. Look up the formula for the mean of the three distributions used in this lab (constant, uniform, exponential). Find the mean for each. Using the average packet interarrival time and packet size, calculate the load which the client is generating (in bits per second).

2. Choose to collect **Node Statistics, Client Print, Traffic Sent (bytes/sec)** and rerun the three scenarios. Did the measured traffic sent match up with the numbers you calculated in Question 1? Why or why not?

3. Look up the formula for the variance of the three distributions used in this lab (constant, uniform, exponential). Find the variance of each. How does the variance of the packet interarrival time affect the buffer usage, queuing delay, and queuing delay variation?

4. Duplicate each scenario, and copy and paste the client to create two clients. Connect the new client to the router. Edit the **File Print (Heavy)** application and double the interarrival times. By doing this, each client will generate half the amount of traffic as shown in the lab exercise, but since there are two clients, the same total amount of traffic will be generated. Rerun the three scenarios, and compare the results (buffer usage, queuing delay, and queuing delay variation) with your original results. Were the results different? If so, why?

5. Duplicate the Uniform scenario, and modify the interarrival time of the **File Print (Heavy)** application. In the lab exercise, the uniform interval is 10 milliseconds wide. Make the interval 20 milliseconds wide and rerun the simulation. Make sure that the mean of the interval is still the same. How does the wider interval affect the results? Repeat for intervals which are 40, 80, 160, and 320 milliseconds wide. Graph your results for the five intervals and explain the behavior you see.

Lab 7   TCP Throughput

Overview
TCP uses a sliding window mechanism to provide flow control. The destination advertises how much space it has available in its buffers, and the source restricts its transmissions so that the receiver is not overloaded. A small flow control window, however, can impact the throughput of the TCP connection. In the extreme, a small flow control window can cause TCP to act like a stop-and-wait protocol. A very large flow control window would allow the TCP source to transmit continuously.

Objective
To examine the throughput of a TCP connection as the flow control window size is varied.

Build the Simulation Model

Start up OPNET IT Guru Academic Edition.
Select the **File** tab => **New...**
Choose **Project** and click on **OK**.
Change the **Project Name** to **xx_TCP_Window_Size** (where **xx** are your initials) and click on **OK**.
In the **Initial Topology** window, select **Create Empty Scenario** and click on **Next**.
In the **Choose Network Scale** window, select **World** and click on **Next**.
In the **Choose Map** window, choose **world** and click on **Next**.
In the **Select Technologies** window, click on **Next**.
In the **Review** window, click on **OK**.

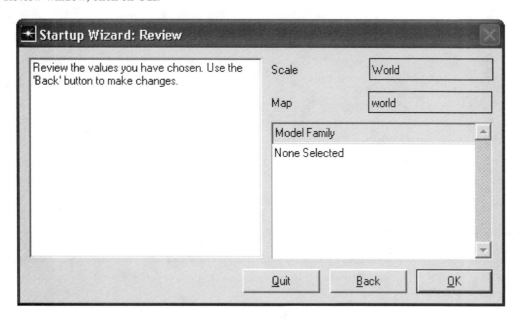

First, it would be helpful to familiarize yourself with the TCP functionality of OPNET.
Select the **Protocols** tab => **TCP** => **Model Usage Guide**. Read through the guide and click on the close window icon to close the PDF viewer when you are done.

Next, we need to configure an application which uses TCP, and associate the application with a profile that will drive our network devices. The File Transfer Protocol (FTP) is built on top of TCP and will serve our purposes.

Select an **Application Config** object from the Object Palette and place it in the project workspace. Right click on the object and choose **Edit Attributes**. Set the **name** attribute to **FTP Application**.

Expand the **Application Definitions** attribute and set the **rows** attribute to **1**. Expand the **row 0** attribute and set the **Name** attribute to **FTP_Large_File**. Expand the **Description** attribute and edit the value of the **Ftp** attribute. Set the **Inter-Request Time (secs)** attribute to **constant(10000)**. Set the **File Size (bytes)** attribute to **constant(1000000)**. In both cases, you will need to set the **Special Value** field to **Not Used** in order to modify the attribute values. The application you have now defined will transfer one 1 MB file at a time so that we can easily analyze the TCP behavior. Click on **OK** to close the window.

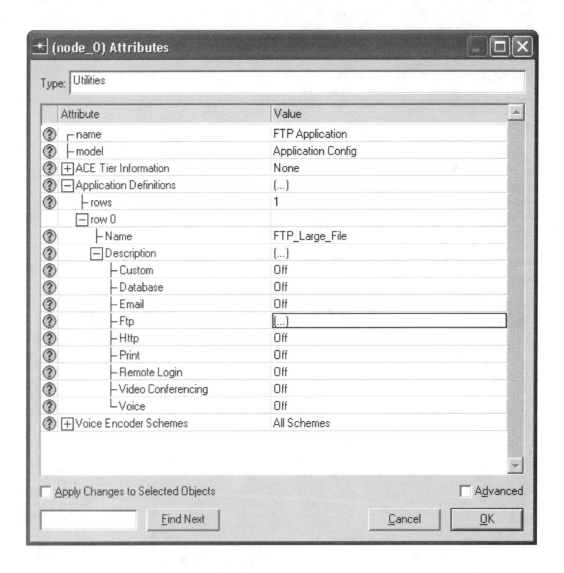

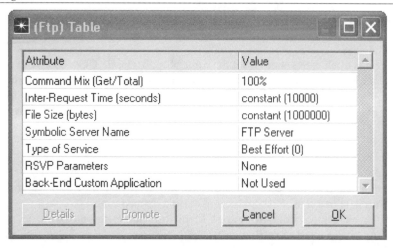

Select a **Profile Config** object from the Object Palette and place it in the project workspace. Right click on the object and choose **Edit Attributes**. Set the **name** attribute to **FTP Profile**.

Expand the **Profile Configuration** attribute and set the **rows** attribute to **1**. Expand the **row 0** attribute and set the **Profile Name** to **FTP_Large_File_Profile**. Expand the **Applications** attribute and set the **rows** attribute to **1**. Expand the **row 0** attribute and set the **Name** to **FTP_Large_File**. Set the **Repeatability** attribute to **Once at Start Time**.

Click on **OK** to close the window.

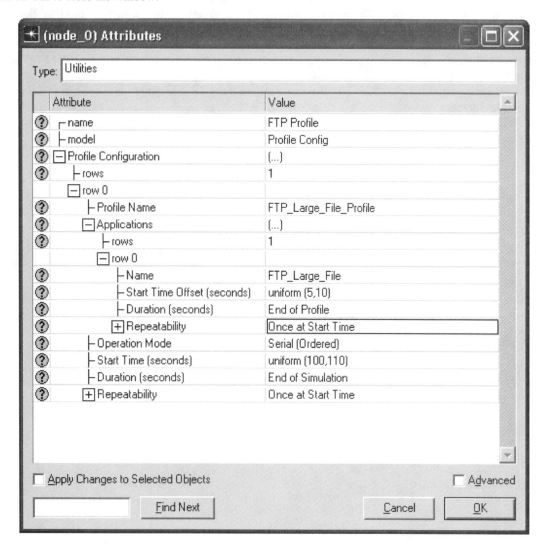

Select an **ip32_cloud** object from the Object Palette and place it in the project workspace. Right click on the cloud and choose **View Node Description**. The cloud represents a WAN consisting of IP-capable routers that supports up to 32 serial links.

Right click on the cloud and select **Set Name**. Set the name to **ip32_cloud**. Click on **OK** to close the window.

Right click on the cloud and select **Edit Attributes**. Set the **Packet Latency (secs)** to **constant(0.25)**. This means that the round-trip delay will be at least 0.5 second. You will need to set the **Special Value** field to **Not Used** in order to modify the latency. Note that the **Packet Discard Ratio** is set to **0.0%**. This means that no losses will occur.

Click on **OK** to close the window.

Select a **ppp_wkstn** device from the Object Palette and place it in the project workspace.

Right click on the station and choose **View Node Description**. Note that the station supports the TCP protocol. We will now set up the client to use the FTP application that we defined.

Right click on the station and choose **Edit Attributes**. Modify the **name** attribute of the device to **FTP Client**.

Edit the **Application: Supported Profiles** attribute. Insert a row and set the **Profile Name** to **FTP_Large_File_Profile**.

Expand the **TCP Parameters** attribute and note that the **Receive Buffer (bytes)** field is set to **8760**. This means that the TCP source may not send more than 8760 bytes of data without receiving an acknowledgment.

Click on **OK** to close the window.

Select a **ppp_server** device from the Object Palette and place in the project workspace.

Right click on the server and choose **View Node Description**. Note that the server supports the TCP protocol. We will now set up the server to use the FTP application that we defined.

Right click on the device and choose **Edit Attributes**. Modify the **name** attribute of the server to **FTP Server**.

Edit the **Application: Supported Services** attribute. Set the **rows** field to **1**. In the first row, set the **Name** to **FTP_Large_File**. Click on **OK** to close the table window.

Expand the **TCP Parameters** attribute and set the **Maximum Segment Size (bytes)** attribute to **512**. This will ensure that each TCP packet sent is 512 bytes long.

Note that the receive buffer size on the server will not affect the TCP throughput as data flow is only in one direction (from server to client).

Click on **OK** to close the window.

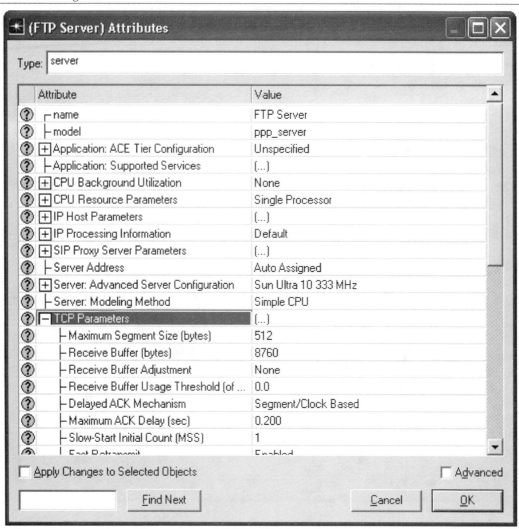

Select a **PPP_DS1** link from the Object Palette and use it to connect the FTP client to the ip32_cloud and the FTP server to the cloud. The PPP protocol is commonly used for long-distance links. Also, remember that DS1 speed is 1.5 Mbps.

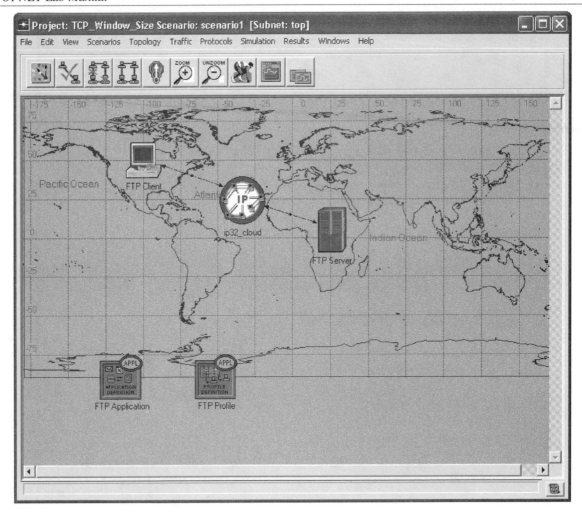

Configure and Run the Simulation

Select the **Simulation** tab => **Choose Individual Statistics...**

Expand the **Global Statistics** item and the **FTP** item, and select the **Download Response Time (sec)** statistic.

Expand the **Node Statistics** item and the **TCP Connection** item, and select the **Sent Segment Sequence Number** and **Traffic Received (bytes/sec)** statistics. Right-click on the **Sent Segment Sequence Number** statistic, and choose **Change Collection Mode**. Click on **Advanced**, and set the **Capture mode** to **all values**. This will ensure that IT Guru will store the sequence number of every packet sent to give us a more detailed graph.

Click on **OK** to close window.

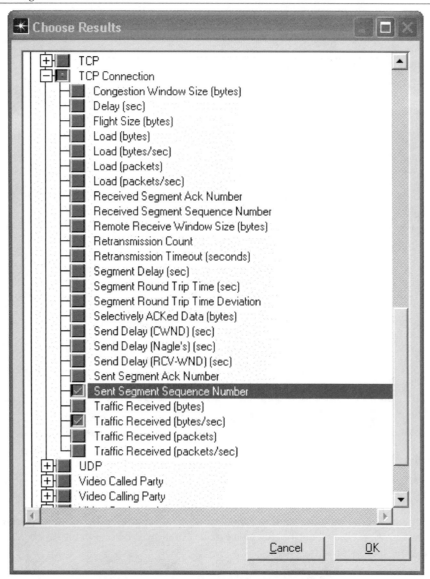

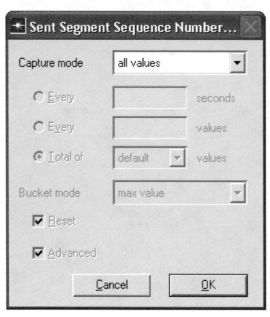

Select **Simulation => Configure Discrete Event Simulation...**
Under the **Common** tab, set the **Duration** to **20**, and the unit to **minute(s)**.
Click on **Run** to run the simulation.
When the simulation has completed, click on **Close** to close the window.

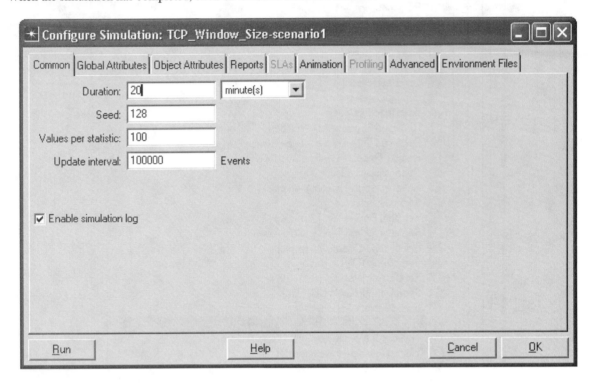

Inspect and Analyze Results

Select the **Results** tab => **View Results...**

Select and expand the **Global Statistics** item and the **Ftp** item, and select the **Download Response Time (sec)** statistic. This statistic shows how long the download took. There will be one point for each file downloaded. Click on the statistic again to disable the preview.

We can calculate the TCP throughput from the download response time. We set the file size to be 1 Mbyte when we configured the FTP application [(1 Mbyte * 8 bits/byte) / 73 seconds = 109.6 Kbps].

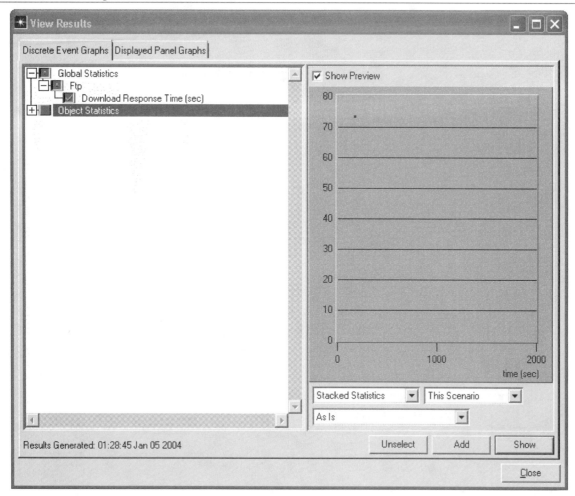

Select and expand the **Object Statistics** item, the **FTP Client** item, and the **TCP Connection** item. Select the **Traffic Received (bytes/sec)** statistic under the FTP Server. You can see the measured throughput over the length of the FTP connection. Note that measured throughput of 14,500 bytes/sec is roughly equal to the throughput we just calculated (14,500 bytes/sec * 8 bits/byte = 116 Kbps). This connection, however, still consumes much less than the capacity of the DS1 lines which connect the server and client to the cloud.

Click on the statistic again to disable the preview.

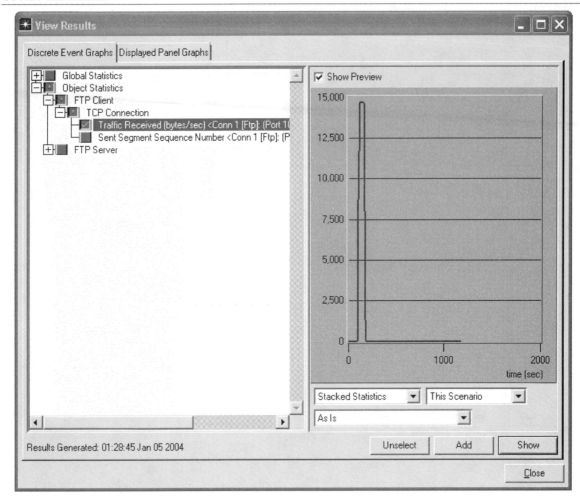

Expand the **Object Statistics**, **FTP Server** and **TCP Connection** items, and select the **Sent Segment Sequence Number** statistic. Click on the **Show** button and expand a small portion of the graph so that you can see more detail. From this graph, you can see the rate at which sequence numbers are used at the source. This rate is directly related to the throughput of the connection. You can also see that the server alternates between periods when it is actively sending (the sequence numbers increase) and periods when it is waiting for acknowledgements from the client (the sequence numbers stay the same). The throughput of this connection is low because the window size is not large enough. The TCP source sends a full window of packets (8 KB), but then must wait for acknowledgements before it can send again.

Note that you may right click on the graph and select **Export Graph Data to Spreadsheet**. This will allow you to examine the actual time value/ sequence number pairs in more detail.

Click on the close window icon and choose to **Delete** the panel to close the statistics window. Click on **Close** to close the results window.

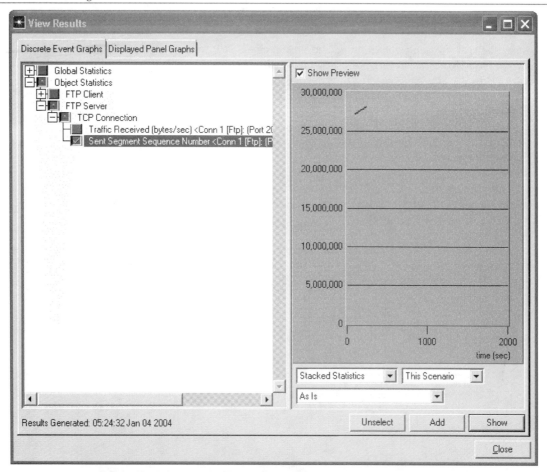

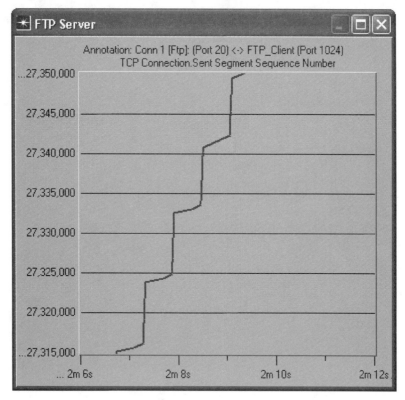

Save your model and close all windows.

Questions

1. Duplicate the scenario and rerun the simulation using client TCP window sizes of 16 KB, 24 KB, 32 KB, 48 KB, and 64 KB. Note the average file download time for each window size. Plot the values using a spreadsheet. How does the window size affect the download time?

2. For the same download times you found in Question 1, calculate the corresponding TCP throughputs.

3. Explain the advantages of implementing a small receive window size. Explain the advantages of implementing a large window size.

4. What would be the effect of increasing the capacity of the lines connecting the server and client to the IP cloud to DS-3 speeds (45 Mbps)? Duplicate the scenario and rerun the simulation to verify your hypothesis and provide statistics to support your answer.

5. What would be the effect of decreasing the capacity of the lines connecting the server and client to the IP cloud to DS-0 speeds (64 Kbps)? Duplicate the scenario and rerun the simulation to verify your hypothesis and provide statistics to support your answer.

Lab 8   TCP Error Control

Overview

In order to correct for segments that have been lost or corrupted, TCP buffers data at the source and does retransmissions when necessary. Typically, losses are detected at the source via a timeout mechanism. If a segment is sent and an acknowledgement is not received before the timer expires, the segment is retransmitted. By default, TCP relies on cumulative acknowledgements. A cumulative acknowledgement for byte **x** acknowledges all bytes less than **x**. Since many segments are sent at once, it is often not clear to the TCP source which segments have been lost. As a result, the TCP source retransmits all unacknowledged segments when a loss is detected (a go-back-n strategy). This strategy may be inefficient if most of the segments actually did arrive at the destination.

An enhancement to TCP to deal with this inefficiency is the Selective Acknowledgment (SACK) option. If both the TCP source and destination agree to use this option, selective acknowledgements are used rather than cumulative. With this specific information regarding loss, the TCP source can do selective repeat retransmissions, i.e., retransmit only the lost segments, rather than all unacknowledged segments.

Objective

To examine the throughput of a TCP connection using the Selective Acknowledgment option when run over a lossy connection.

Build the Simulation Model

Start up OPNET IT Guru Academic Edition.
Select the **File** tab => **New...**
Choose **Project** and click on **OK**.
Change the **Project Name** to **xx_TCP_SACK** (where **xx** are your initials) and click on **OK**.
In the **Initial Topology** window, select **Create Empty Scenario** and click on **Next**.
In the **Choose Network Scale** window, select **Choose from Maps** and click on **Next**.
In the **Choose Map** window, choose **california** and click on **Next**.
In the **Select Technologies** window, click on **Next**.
In the **Review** window, click on **OK**.

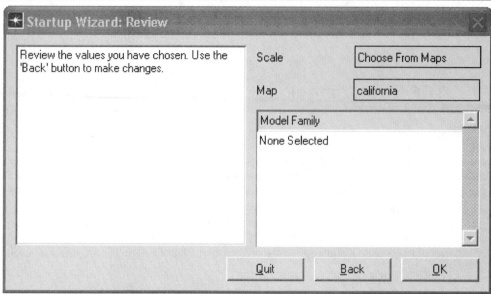

First, it would be helpful to familiarize yourself with the TCP functionality of OPNET.

Select the **Protocols** tab => **TCP** => **Model Usage Guide**. Read through the guide and click on the close window icon to close the PDF viewer when you are done.

Next, we need to configure an application which uses TCP, and associate the application with a profile that will drive our network devices. The HyperText Transfer Protocol (HTTP) is built on top of TCP and will serve our purposes.

Select an **Application Config** object from the Object Palette and place it in the project workspace. Right click on the object and choose **Edit Attributes**. Set the **name** attribute to **HTTP Application**.

Expand the **Application Definitions** attribute and set the **rows** attribute to **1**. Expand the **row 0** attribute and set the **Name** attribute to **HTTP_Large_File**. Expand the **Description** attribute and edit the value of the **Http** attribute. Set the **Page Interarrival Time (secs)** attribute to **constant(10000)**. Click on the **Page Properties** value field to bring up the **(Page Properties) Table** window. Set the **Object Size (bytes)** attribute to **constant(1000000)** and the **Number of Objects...** to **constant(1)**. You will need to set the **Special Value** field to **Not Used** in order to modify these values. The application you have now defined will transfer one 1-MB file at a time so that we can easily analyze the TCP behavior.

Click on **OK** three times to close the three windows.

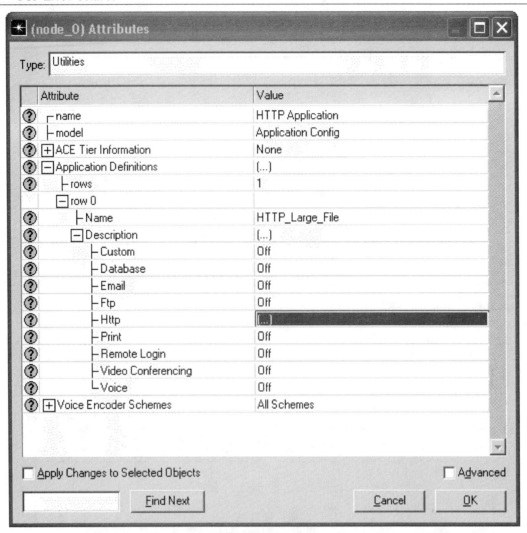

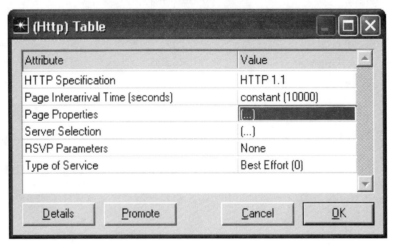

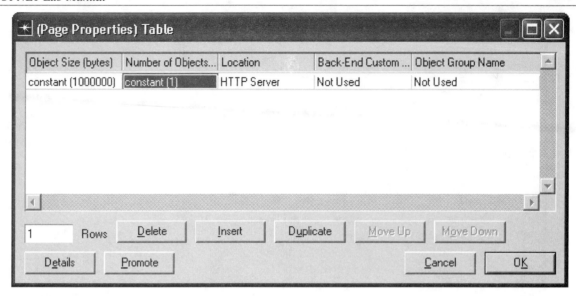

Select a **Profile Config** object from the Object Palette and place it in the project workspace. Right click on the object and choose **Edit Attributes**. Set the **name** attribute to **HTTP Profile**.

Expand the **Profile Configuration** attribute and set the **rows** attribute to **1**. Expand the **row 0** attribute and set the **Profile Name** to **HTTP_Large_File_Profile**. Expand the **Applications** attribute and set the **rows** attribute to **1**. Expand the **row 0** attribute and set the **Name** to **HTTP_Large_File**. Set the **Repeatability** attribute to **Once at Start Time**.

Click on **OK** to close the window.

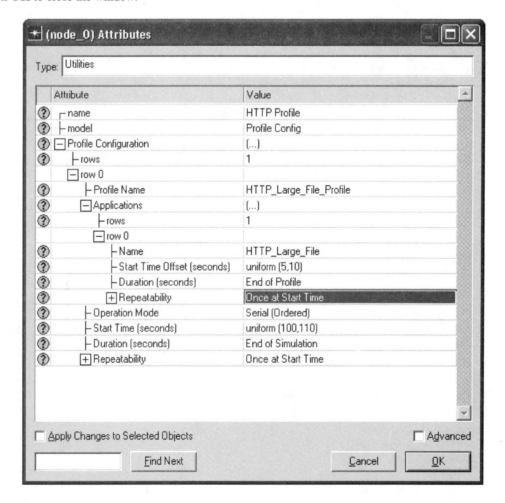

Select an **ip32_cloud** object from the Object Palette and place it in the project workspace. Right click on the cloud and choose **View Node Description**. The cloud represents a WAN consisting of IP-capable that supports up to 32 serial links

Right click on the cloud and select **Set Name**. Set the name to **ip32_cloud**. Click on OK to close the window.

Right click on the cloud and select **Edit Attributes**. Set the **Packet Discard Ratio** to **1%**. This means that 1 in 100 packets will be discarded as they pass through the WAN and retransmissions will be required.

Set the **Packet Latency (secs)** to **constant(0.25)**. This means that the round-trip delay will be at least 0.5 second. You will need to set the **Special Value** field to **Not Used** in order to modify the latency.

Click on **OK** to close the window.

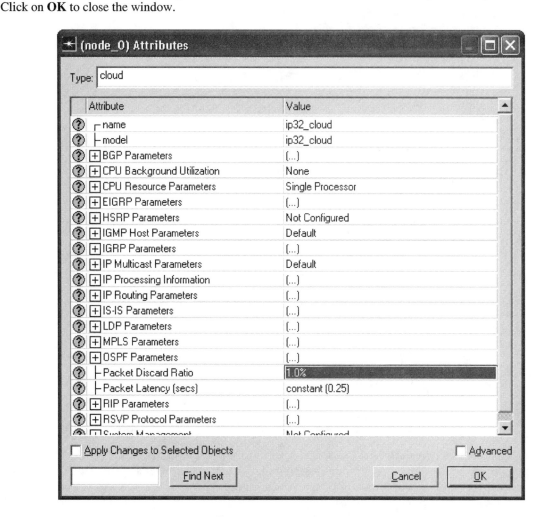

Select a **ppp_wkstn** device from the Object Palette and place it in the project workspace.

Right click on the station and choose **View Node Description**. Note that the station supports the TCP protocol. We will now set up the client to use the HTTP application that we defined.

Right click on the station and choose **Edit Attributes**. Modify the **name** attribute of the device to **HTTP Client**.

Edit the **Application: Supported Profiles** attribute. Insert a row and set the **Profile Name** to **HTTP_Large_File_Profile**.

Expand the **TCP Parameters** attribute and set the **Selective ACK (SACK)** attribute to **enabled**. Set the **Fast Retransmit** and **Fast Recovery** attributes to **disabled**. Fast Retransmit and Fast Recovery are alternate TCP error control mechanisms. By disabling them, we can concentrate on the effects of the SACK mechanism.

Click on **OK** to close the window.

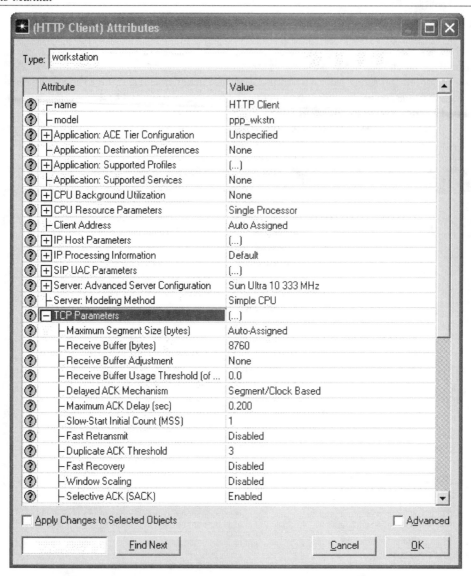

Select a **ppp_server** device from the Object Palette and place it in the project workspace.

Right click on the server and choose **View Node Description**. Note that the server supports the TCP protocol. We will now set up the server to support the HTTP application that we defined.

Right click on the device and choose **Edit Attributes**. Modify the **name** attribute of the server to **HTTP Server**.

Edit the **Application: Supported Services** attribute. Set the **rows** field to **1**. In the first row, set the **Name** to **HTTP_Large_File**. Click on **OK** to close the table window.

Expand the **TCP Parameters** attribute and set the **Maximum Segment Size (bytes)** attribute to **512**. This will ensure that each TCP packet sent is 512 bytes long.

Set the **Selective ACK (SACK)** attribute to **enabled**. Set the **Fast Retransmit** and **Fast Recovery** attributes to **disabled**.

Click on **OK** to close the window.

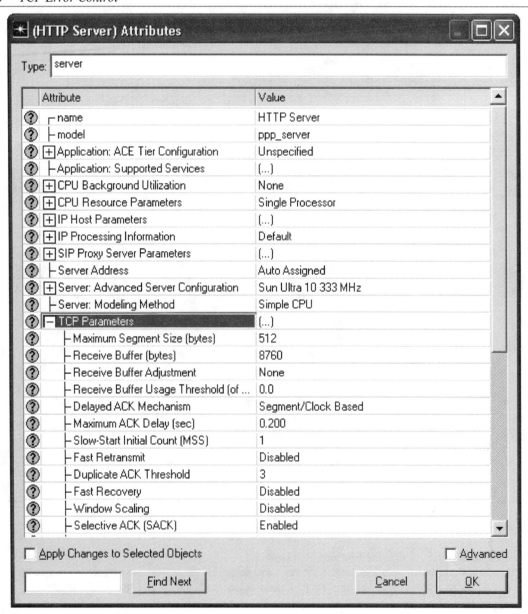

Select a **PPP_DS1** link from the Object Palette and use it to connect the HTTP client to the ip32_cloud. Use another to connect the HTTP server to the cloud. The PPP protocol is commonly used for long-distance links. Also, remember that DS1 speed is 1.5 Mbps.

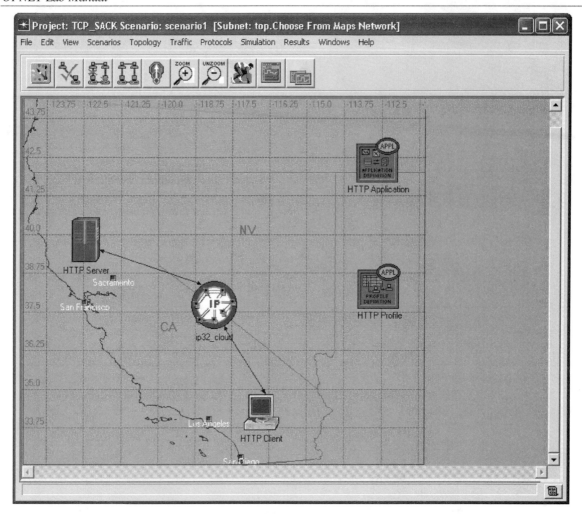

Configure and Run the Simulation

Select the **Simulation** tab => **Choose Individual Statistics...**
Expand the **Global Statistics** item and the **HTTP** item, and select the **Page Response Time (sec)** statistic.
Expand the **Node Statistics** item and the **TCP Connection** item, and select the **Retransmission Count**, **Selectively ACKed Data (bytes)**, and **Sent Segment Sequence Number** statistics. Right-click on the **Sent Segment Sequence Number** statistic, and choose **Change Collection Mode**. Click on **Advanced** and set the **Capture mode** to **all values**. This will ensure that IT Guru will store the sequence number of every packet sent to give us a more detailed graph.
Click on **OK** to close the window.

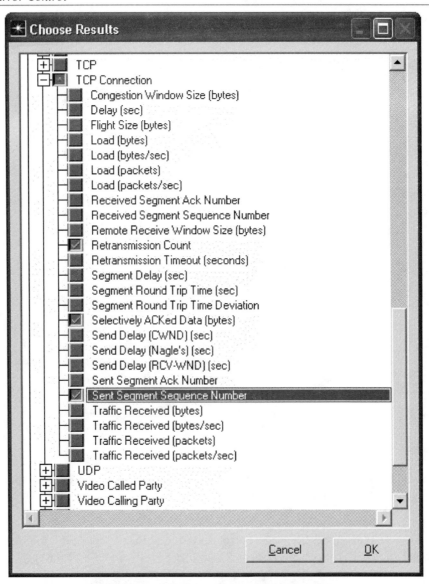

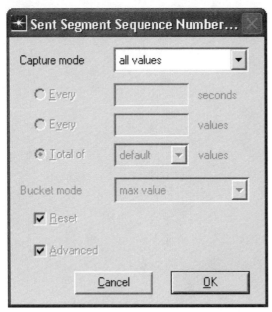

Select **Simulation => Configure Discrete Event Simulation...**
Under the **Common** tab, set the **Duration** to **5**, and the unit to **minute(s)**.
Click on **Run** to run the simulation.
When the simulation has completed, click on **Close** to close the window.

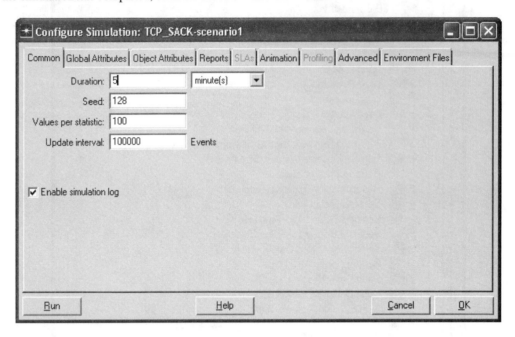

Inspect and Analyze Results

Select the **Results** tab => **View Results...**

Select and expand the **Global Statistics** item and the **Http** item, and select the **Page Response Time (sec)** statistic. This statistic shows how long the download took. There will be one point for each page downloaded. Click on the statistic again to disable the preview.

We can calculate the TCP throughput from the download response time. We set the file size to be 1 Mbyte when we configured the HTTP application [(1 Mbyte * 8 bits/byte) / 145 seconds = 55.2 Kbps].

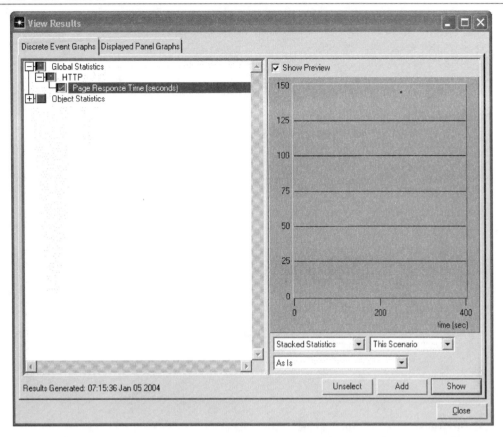

Select and expand the **Object Statistics** item, the **Choose From Maps Network** item, the **HTTP Server** item, and the **TCP Connection** item. Select the **Selectively ACKed Data (bytes)** statistic. This graph shows how much data was selectively acknowledged as opposed to being acknowledged via the standard cumulative acknowledgment mechanism. You can see that a fair amount of data is selectively acknowledged at any time during the transfer indicating that the SACK mechanism is performing a useful service to the TCP source (the HTTP server in this case).

Click on the statistic again to disable the preview.

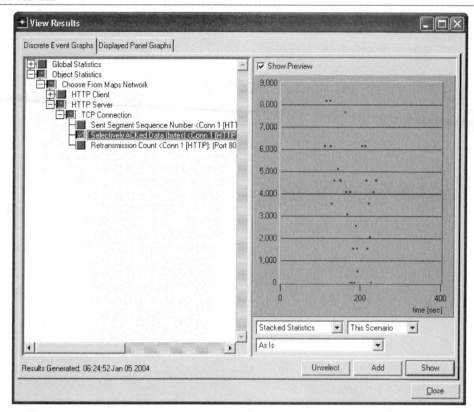

Now select the **Retransmission Count** statistic. From this graph, you can see that many retransmissions were required. When using the SACK option, these retransmissions may be done more efficiently.
Click on the statistic again to disable the preview.

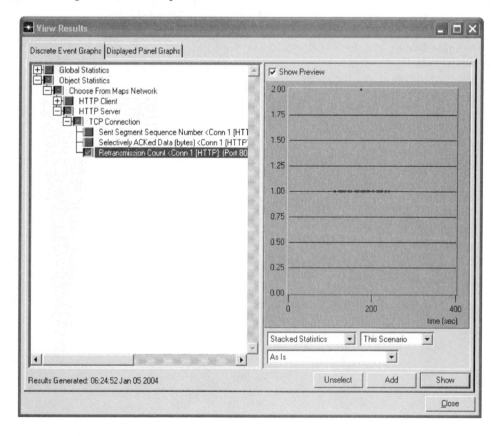

Finally, select the **Sent Segment Sequence Number** statistic. Click on the **Show** button and expand a small portion of the graph so that you can see more detail. From this graph, you can see that, while the throughput is not constant, the TCP source quickly recovers from errors. There are few or no spots in the graph where the sequence numbers do not increase.

Note that you may right click on the graph and select **Export Graph Data to Spreadsheet**. This will allow you to examine the actual time value/ sequence number pairs in more detail.

Click on the close window icon and choose to **Delete** the panel to close the statistics window. Click on **Close** to close the results window.

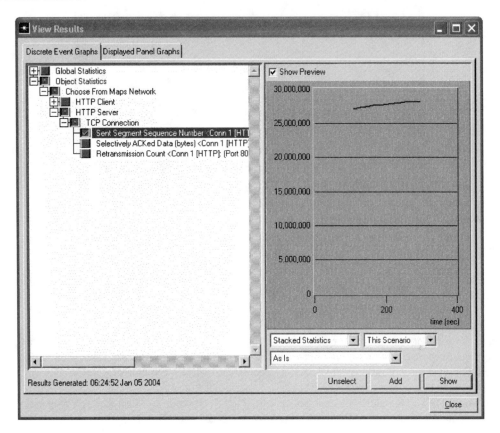

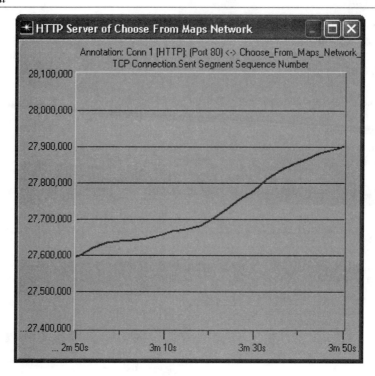

Save your model and close all windows.

Questions

1. Duplicate the scenario and modify the HTTP Client and HTTP Server TCP Connection attributes to disable Selective Acknowledgements. Rerun the simulation and record the HTTP Page Response Time. Calculate the associated TCP throughput. Does the change improve or degrade the response time and throughput?

2. Duplicate the scenario and repeat the simulation with Packet Discard Ratios of 0.0%, 0.5%, 5%, and 10%. Record the Page Response Time and, together with your results using a 1% discard ratio, plot the values using a spreadsheet. For what discard ratios is the SACK mechanism effective? Explain why.

3. Two additional TCP error control mechanisms are the Fast Retransmit and Fast Recovery schemes, which are usually implemented together. Duplicate the scenario and disable the SACK option on the HTTP server and HTTP Client. Set the discard rate to 1% in the ip32_cloud. Modify the values of the Fast Retransmit and Fast Recovery attributes under the TCP Parameters attribute on both the client and server. They should be set to enabled, and Reno respectively. Run the simulation and record the Page Response Time. Disable the Fast Retransmit and Fast Recovery attributes and rerun the simulation. Record the Page Response Time. How did the error control mechanisms affect the response time?

4. Compare the Page Response Time for three scenarios:
        a) Selective Acknowledgements only,
        b) Fast Retransmit and Fast Recovery only,
        c) Selective Acknowledgements combined with Fast Retransmit and Fast Recovery.

Which scenario gives the best results? Why do you think this is so?

Lab 9   TCP versus UDP Response Time

Overview

TCP provides connection-oriented service at the transport layer, and UDP provides connectionless service. As a result, a data exchange using TCP can take longer than the same exchange using UDP. TCP implementations require that the TCP source and destination perform a three-way handshake in order to set up the connection prior to sending data, and a four-way handshake when tearing down the connection. In addition, all data must be acknowledged by the destination when it is received. UDP sources, on the other hand, do not set up connections and so save the overhead in terms of delay and bandwidth usage. UDP is often used when small amounts of data must be sent, for example, when doing credit card verification. If large amounts of data are sent, however, the extra TCP overhead may be negligible in comparison to the entire transaction completion time.

Objective

To examine the response time for large and small data transfers when using TCP and UDP.

Build the Simulation Model

Start up OPNET IT Guru Academic Edition.
Select the **File** tab => **New...**
Choose **Project** and click on **OK**.
Change the **Project Name** to **xx_TCP_vs_UDP** (where **xx** are your initials). Set the **Scenario Name** to **TCP** and click on **OK**.
In the **Initial Topology** window, select **Create Empty Scenario** and click on **Next**.
In the **Choose Network Scale** window, select **World** and click on **Next**.
In the **Choose Map** window, choose **world** and click on **Next**.
In the **Select Technologies** window, click on **Next**.
In the **Review** window, click on **OK**.

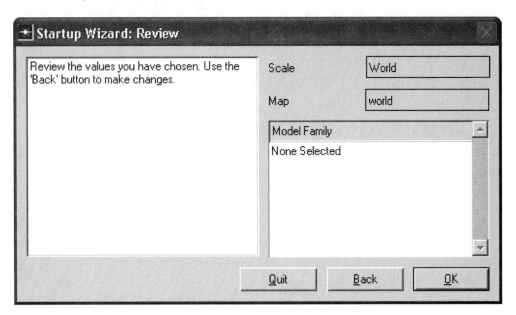

First, it would be helpful to familiarize yourself with the TCP functionality of OPNET and with the methods for defining new applications.

Select the **Protocols** tab => **TCP** => **Model Usage Guide**. Read through the guide and click on the close window icon to close the PDF viewer when you are done.

Select the **Protocols** tab => **Applications** => **Model Usage Guides** => **Configuring Profiles and Applications**. Read through the guide and click on the close window icon to close the PDF viewer when you are done.

Next, we will create a client-server system running over a wide area network.

Select an **ip32_cloud** object from the Object Palette and place it in the project workspace. Right click on the cloud and choose **View Node Description**. The cloud represents a WAN consisting of IP-capable that supports up to 32 serial links.

Right click on the cloud and select **Set Name**. Set the name to **ip32_cloud**. Click on **OK** to close the window.

In the Object Palette, click on **Configure Palette**. Click on **Node Models**, and choose to include the **ppp_wkstn_adv** model. Click on **OK** twice and save your palette with the default name given when the **Save As** window comes up.

Select a **ppp_wkstn_adv** device from the Object Palette and place it in the project workspace.

Right click on the station and choose **View Node Description**. Note that the station supports the TCP and UDP protocols.

Right click on the station and choose **Edit Attributes**. Modify the **name** attribute of the device to **Application Client**.

Modify the **Client Address** to be **Application Client** as well.

Click on **OK** to close the window.

Select a **ppp_server** device from the Object Palette and place it in the project workspace.

Right click on the server and choose **View Node Description**. Note that the server supports the TCP and UDP protocols.

Right click on the device and choose **Edit Attributes**. Modify the **name** attribute of the server to **Application Server**.

Modify the **Server Address** to be **Application Server** as well.

Click on **OK** to close the window.

Select two **PPP_DS1** links from the Object Palette and use them to connect the **Application Client** to the ip32_cloud and the **Application Server** to the cloud. The PPP protocol is commonly used for long-distance links. Also, remember that DS1 speed is 1.5 Mbps.

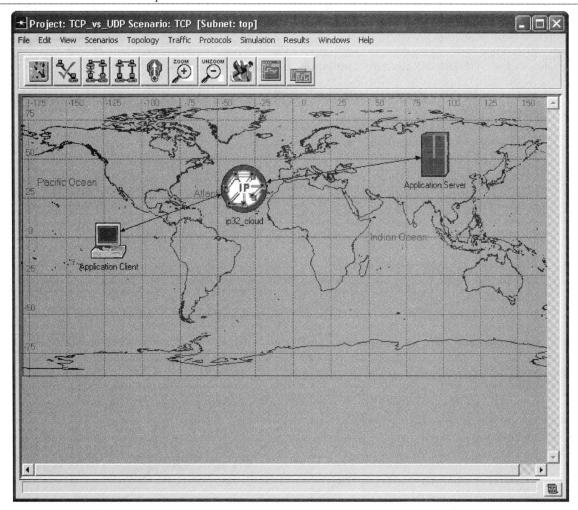

Now we will create a custom application which can run on top of either TCP or UDP. The application will require that the client send a single request to the server and that the server reply with a single response. A task definition must be created that will be used to define an application. That application will then be incorporated into a profile that we can associate with our client and server.

Select a **Task Config** object from the Object Palette and place it in the project workspace. Right click on the object and choose **Edit Attributes**. Set the **name** attribute to **Task**.
Expand the **Task Specification** attribute and set the **rows** attribute to **1**. Expand the **row 0** attribute and set the **Task Name** attribute to **Request_Response_Task**. Now edit the **Manual Configuration** attribute to define the task. Set the number of **rows** to **1**. Edit the **Phase Name** and set it to **Only_Phase**. Click on **OK** to close the window.

Set the **Source** to be **Application Client**. Set the **Destination** to be **Application Server**. Edit the **Source->Dest Traffic** field, and set the **Initialization Time** to **constant(0)**, the **Request Count** to **constant(1)**, the **Interrequest Time (seconds)** to **constant(1.0)**, and the **Packets per Request** to **constant(1).** Click on **OK** to close the window. This task will cause the client to send one request packet every second.

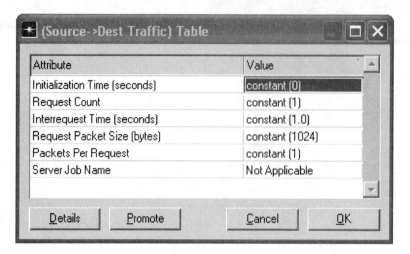

Edit the **Dest->Source Traffic** field, and set the **Interresponse Time** to **constant(0)**. Click on **OK** to close the window. This task will cause the server to respond to requests immediately with a single application-layer packet.

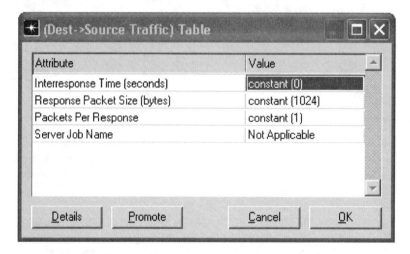

Edit the **Transport Connection** field, and set the **Policy** to **New Connection per Request**. Click on **OK** three times to complete the task configuration.

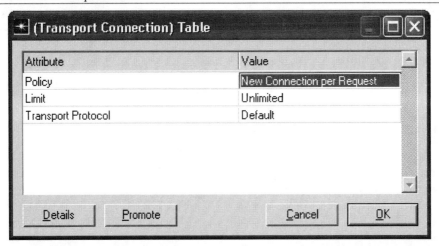

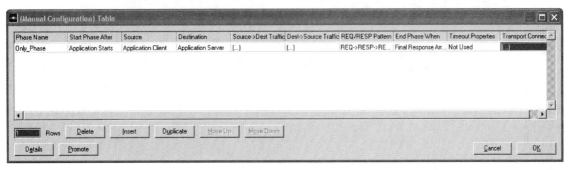

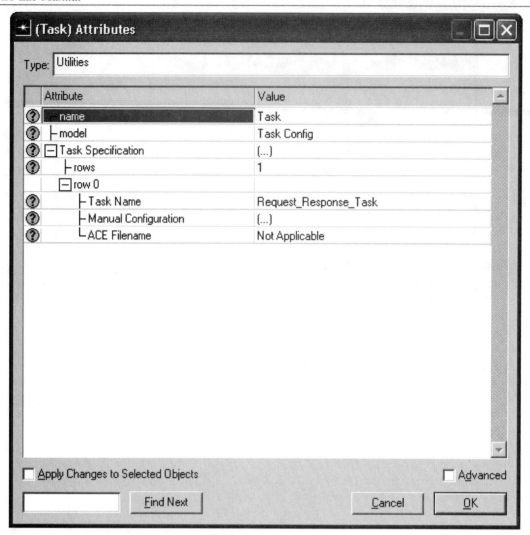

Right click on the **Application Config** object that appeared in the project workspace when we completed the task definition, and choose **Edit Attributes**. Set the **name** attribute to **Application**.

Expand the **Application Definitions** attribute and set the **rows** attribute to **1**. Expand the **row 0** attribute and set the **Name** attribute to **Request_Response_Application**. Expand the **Description** attribute and edit the value of the **Custom** attribute. Note that the **Transport Protocol** is currently set to **TCP**. Edit the **Task Description** attribute. Set the number of **rows** to **1**. Set the **Task Name** to **Request_Response_Task**. Click on **OK** three times to close the windows and complete the custom application configuration.

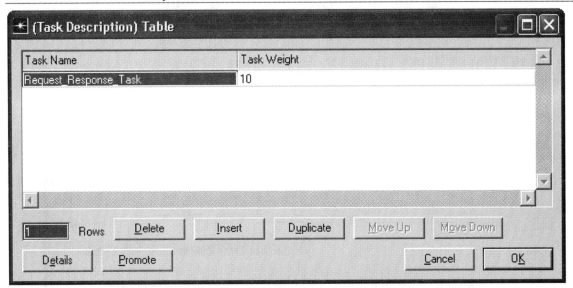

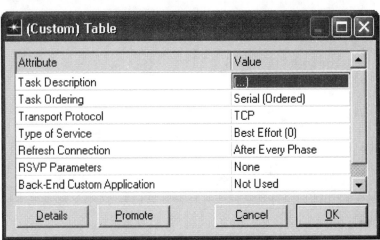

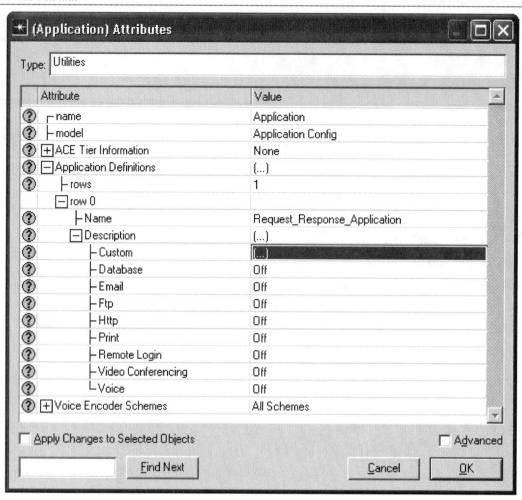

Select a **Profile Config** object from the Object Palette and place it in the project workspace. Right click on the object and choose **Edit Attributes**. Set the **name** attribute to **Profile**.

Expand the **Profile Configuration** attribute and set the **rows** attribute to **1**. Expand the **row 0** attribute and set the **Profile Name** to **Request_Response_Profile**. Expand the **Applications** attribute and set the **rows** attribute to **1**. Expand the **row 0** attribute and set the **Name** to **Request_Response_Application**. Set the **Duration (seconds)** to **End of Last Task**. Expand the **Repeatability** attribute and set the **Inter-repetition Time (seconds)** to **constant(30)**. Set the **Start Time (seconds)** to **constant(5)**. Expand the second **Repeatability** item, in the main level hierarchy, and set the **Inter-repetition Time (seconds)** to **constant(30)** and the **Number of Repetitions** to **constant(1)**. Click on **O K** to close the window. This profile will cause the **Request_Response_Application** to run every 30 seconds.

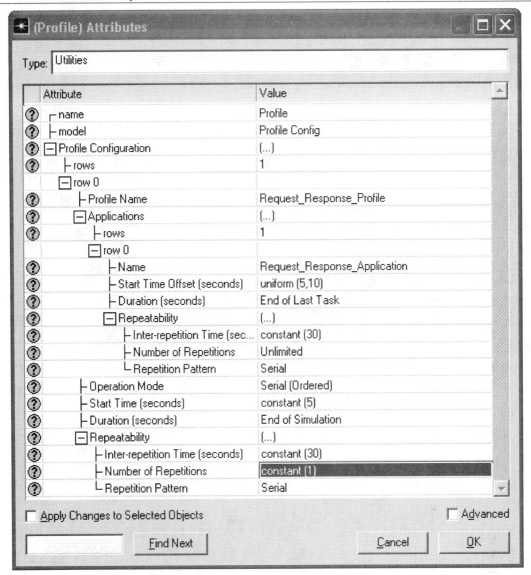

Now we will associate our custom application with our client and server. Right click on the **Application Client** and choose **Edit Attributes**. Edit the **Application: Supported Profiles** attribute. Set **rows** to **1**, and expand the **row 0** attribute. Set the **Profile Name** to **Request_Response_Profile**. Edit the **Application: Destination Preferences** attribute. Set the number of **rows** to **1**, and the **Symbolic Name** to **Application Server**. Edit the **Actual Name** field, set the number of **rows** to **1**, and set the **Name** to **Application Server**. Click on **OK** twice to close the windows. Edit the **Application: Source Preferences** attribute, set the number of **rows** to **1**, and set the **Symbolic Name** to **Application Client**. Click on **OK** to close the window.

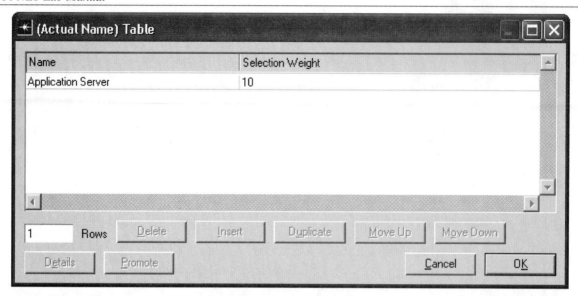

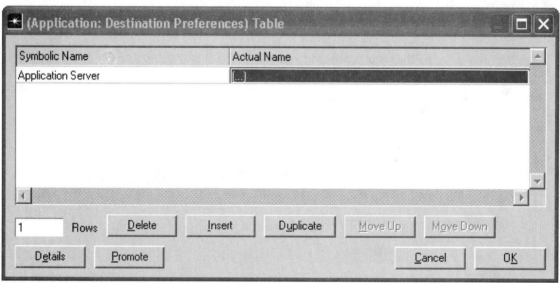

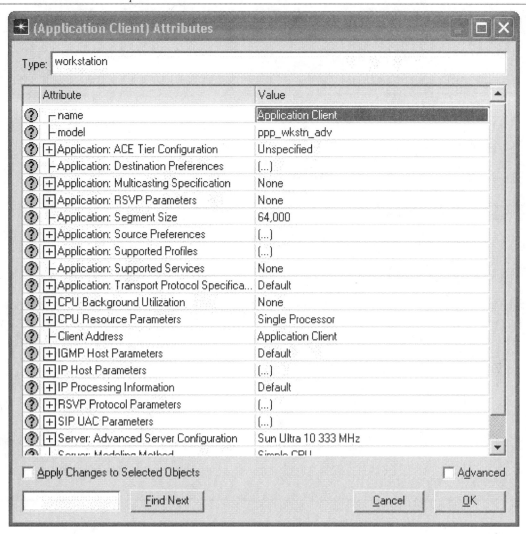

Right click on the Application Server and choose **Edit Attributes**. Edit the **Application: Supported Services** attribute. Set **rows** to **1**, and set the **Name** to **Request_Response_Application**. Click on **OK** twice to close the windows.

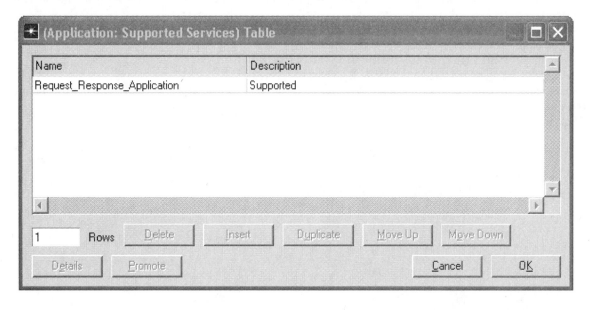

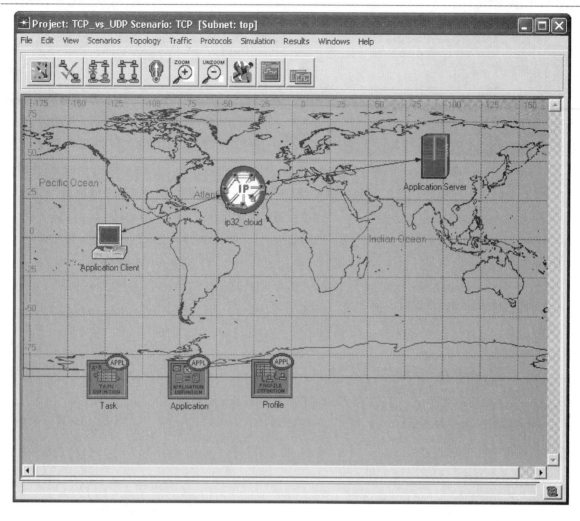

Configure the Simulation

Select the **Simulation** tab => **Choose Individual Statistics...**
Expand the **Global Statistics** item and the **Custom Application** item, and select the **Task Response Time (seconds)** statistic.
Expand the **Node Statistics** item and the **IP** item, and select the **Traffic Received (packets/sec)** and **Traffic Sent (packets/sec)** statistics.
Expand the **TCP** item and select the **Traffic Received (packets/sec).**
Expand the **UDP item** and select the **Traffic Received (packets/sec).**
Expand the **Link Statistics**, and the **point-to-point** item, and select **throughput (bits/sec) -->** and **throughput (bits/sec) <--.**
Click on **OK** to close window.

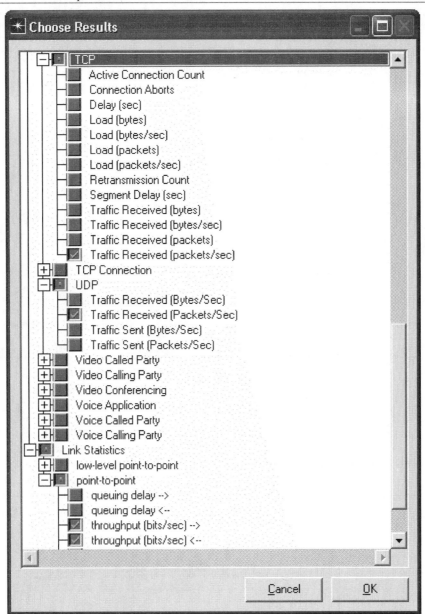

Select **Simulation => Configure Discrete Event Simulation...**
Under the **Common** tab, set the **Duration** to **1**, and the unit to **hour(s)**.
Click on **OK** to close the window.

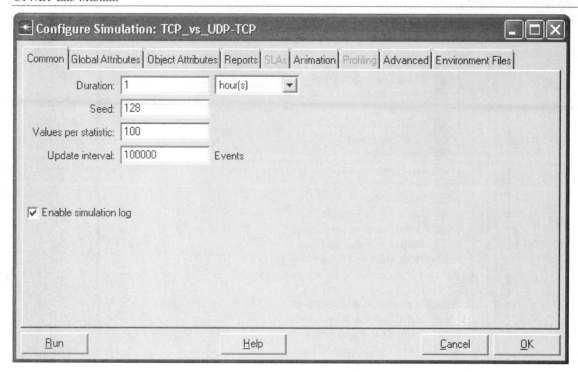

Duplicate the Scenario

We are now going to duplicate the scenario and configure the application to use UDP instead. This will allow us to compare the performance of the application across the two transport layer protocols. Choose **Scenarios => Duplicate Scenario**, and name the new scenario **UDP**.

Right click on the **Application Config** object, expand the **Application Definitions** item, the **row 0** item, and the **Description** item. Edit the **Custom** application definition, and modify the **Transport Protocol** to **UDP**. Click on **OK** twice to close the windows.

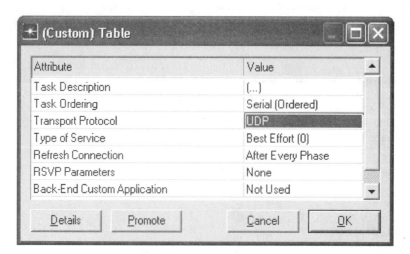

Run the Simulation

Select the **Scenarios** tab => **Manage Scenarios...**
Edit **Results** field in both rows and set the value to **<collect>** or **<recollect>**.
Click on **OK** to run both scenarios (one after the other).

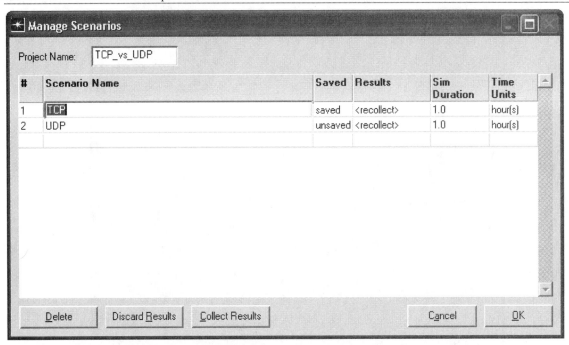

When the simulation has completed, click on **Close** to close the window.

Inspect and Analyze Results

Select the **Results** tab => **Compare Results...**

Select and expand the **Global Statistics** item and the **Custom Application** item, and select the **Task Response Time (seconds)** statistic. This statistic shows how long each task took to complete. Use **As Is** mode to view the statistic. Click on **Show** to see a more detailed graph. There will be one point for each time the application was run and one set of points for TCP and another for UDP. You can see that the application took nearly twice as long to complete each task when using TCP as it did when using UDP. This is likely due to the lack of connection setup and teardown delay in UDP. Click on the close window icon and **Delete** the panel. Click on the statistic again to disable the preview.

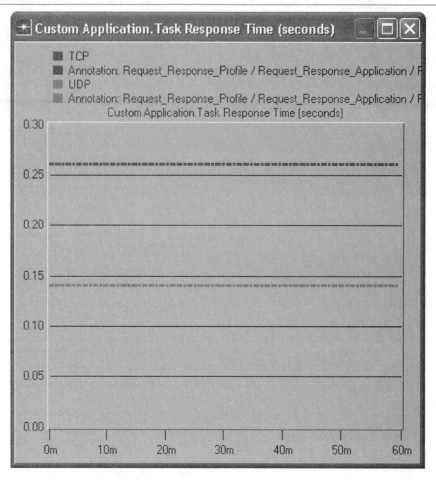

Select and expand the **Object Statistics** item, the **Application Client** item, and the **IP** item. Select the **Traffic Received (packets/sec)** statistic and use **average** mode to view the statistic. Click on **Show**. You can see the client received a larger number of packets per second in the TCP case than the UDP case, nearly five times as many. This is due to the need to set up connections and tear them down again in the TCP case. Click on the close window icon and **Delete** the panel. Click on the statistic again to disable the preview.

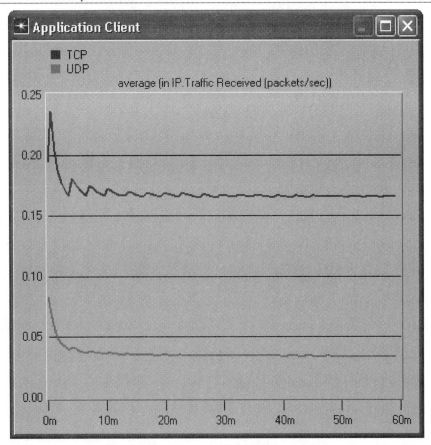

Expand the **Application Client <-> ip32_cloud[0]** item, the **point-to-point** item, and select the **throughput (bits/sec) -->** statistic. Use **average** mode to view the statistic. Click on **Show**. This statistic shows the amount of traffic that was seen on the link between the client and the WAN. Even though the same number of requests and responses were executed in both scenarios, the bandwidth usage is less in the UDP case. This is again due to the fact that UDP does not need to send connection setup and teardown packets. Click on the close window icon and **Delete** the panel. Click on **Close** to close the **View Results** window.

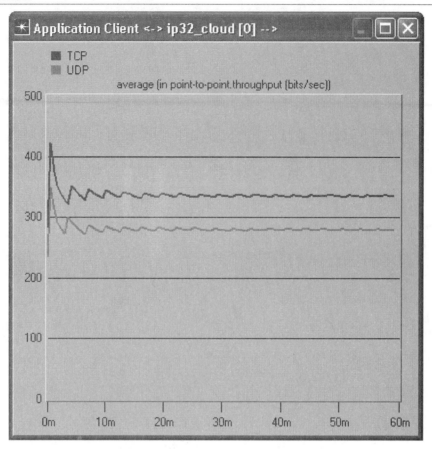

Save your model and close all windows.

Questions

1. Based on the configuration parameters, what would the throughput on the links be if there were no control packets (such as connection setup and teardown packets)? You can use the values you set in the Task Configuration and Profile Configuration objects to calculate an answer. Look for the size of the request, the size of the response, and the delay between requests.

2. Based on your answer to Question 1, and the results from your simulation, how much overhead did UDP impose? In other words, what percentage of the bytes sent on the links was used for packet headers and control packets? How much overhead did TCP impose?

3. Duplicate your scenarios and modify the **Dest --> Source Traffic** in the **Task Specification** for both UDP and TCP scenarios so that the **Packets per Response** is **constant(1000)** instead. This configuration corresponds to an application which sends a small request and then receives a large file in response. Calculate the size of the response. Now rerun the simulation for both scenarios. How much slower is the **Task Response** time when using TCP than when using UDP? How large must the responses be before the TCP response time is less than 10% longer than the UDP response time?

4. Switch to the small packet request-response scenario. Duplicate the scenario and edit the attributes of the **ip32_cloud** to modify the **Packet Discard Ratio** to **1%**. Rerun the simulation. How does error affect the response time for UDP and TCP? Explain your results.

5. Investigate the operation of TCP. Explain how connection setup is accomplished. Explain how connection teardown is accomplished. Draw diagrams to illustrate your explanations.

Lab 10   Firewall Performance

Overview
A firewall is a router which provides additional security functionality. They are commonly deployed at the border of a corporate network and the Internet, and are used to monitor and regulate the traffic that passes through this border. Firewalls inspect various header fields in packets as they arrive and, based on a security policy, choose to discard (filter) the packets, or forward them on to the destination. Packets may be filtered based on the source or destination IP address, the source or destination port number, or other header fields. For instance, a corporate site's firewall could be configured to accept only packets originating at the corporation's other locations, or only packets destined for the FTP port. All other packets would be discarded to protect the corporation's devices from unwanted access. While firewalls provide a valuable service, the additional filtering functionality can require extra processing time, possibly lowering throughput.

Objective
To examine the effect of firewall filtering on application response time.

Build the Simulation Model

Start up OPNET IT Guru Academic Edition.
Select the **File** tab => **New...**
Choose **Project** and click on **OK**.
Change the **Project Name** to **xx_Firewall** (where **xx** are your initials). Set the **Scenario Name** to **No_Firewall** and click on **OK**.
In the **Initial Topology** window, select **Create Empty Scenario** and click on **Next**.
In the **Choose Network Scale** window, select **World** and click on **Next**.
In the **Choose Map** window, choose **usa** and click on **Next**.
In the **Select Technologies** window, click on **Next**.
In the **Review** window, click on **OK**.

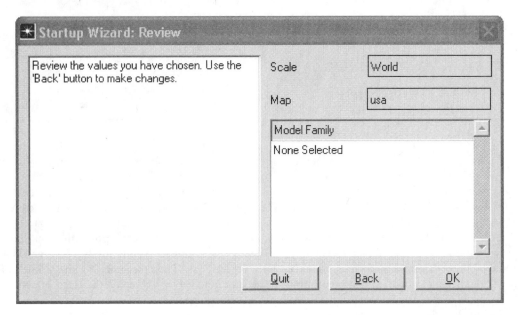

First, we will configure the traffic profiles for our users. We need one profile for the motivated workers, who will perform database transactions, and one profile for the idle workers, who will do web browsing.

Select an **Application Config** object from the Object Palette and place it in the project workspace. Right click on the object and choose **Edit Attributes**. Set the **name** to **Applications**. Set the **Application Definitions** attribute to **Default**. We can now use or modify the default applications defined by OPNET, including web browsing, FTP, and others.

Expand the **Application Definitions** attribute and the **row 0** attribute (which describes the **Database Access (Heavy)** application). Expand the **Description** attribute and modify the **Database** attribute to **High Load**. Click on **OK** to close the window.

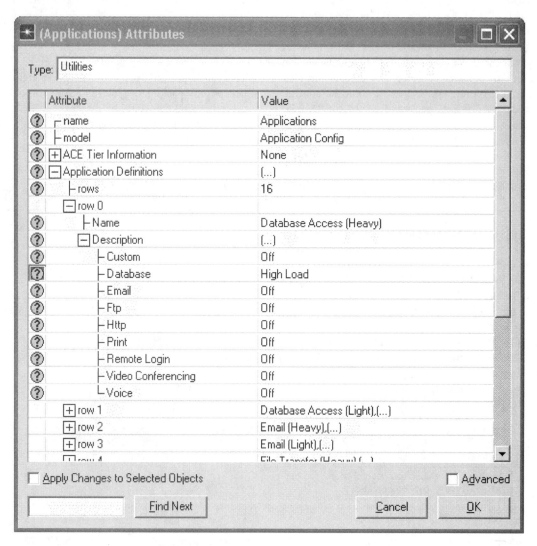

Select a **Profile Config** object from the Object Palette and place it in the project workspace. Right click on the object and choose **Edit Attributes**. Set the **name** to **Profiles**. Expand the **Profile Configuration** attribute and set the **rows** attribute to **2**. Expand the **row 0** attribute, and set the **Profile Name** to **Database_User**. Expand the **Applications** attribute, and set the **rows** attribute to **1**. Expand the **row 0** attribute, and set the **Name** to **Database Access (Heavy)**. Set the **Start Time Offset (seconds)** to **exponential(12)**. Set the **Start Time (seconds)** for the profile (which is the second Start Time attribute) to **exponential(20)**.

Expand the **row 1** attribute, and set the **Profile Name** to **Web_User**. Expand the **Applications** attribute , and set the **rows** attribute to **1**. Expand the **row 0** attribute, and set the **Name** to **Web Browsing (Heavy HTTP1.1)**. Set the **Start Time Offset (seconds)** to **exponential(60)**. Set the **Start Time (seconds)** for the profile (which is the second Start Time attribute) to **exponential(60)**. The start time values will cause the large number of users (100) to be spread over a long interval so that they do not all start at once.

Click on **OK** to close the window.

Now, we will create a client–server system running over a wide area network, with the clients in the West and the servers in the East.

Select an **ip32_cloud** object from the Object Palette and place it in the project workspace. Right click on the cloud and choose **View Node Description**. The cloud represents a WAN consisting of IP-capable routers that supports up to 32 serial links
Right click on the cloud and select **Edit Attributes**. Set the name to **ip32_cloud**. Set the **Packet Latency (secs)** to **constant(0.05)**. You will need to change the **Special Value** to **Not Used** in order to modify the Packet Latency value. Any packet which passes through the cloud will now experience a delay of 50 milliseconds. Click on **OK** to close the window.

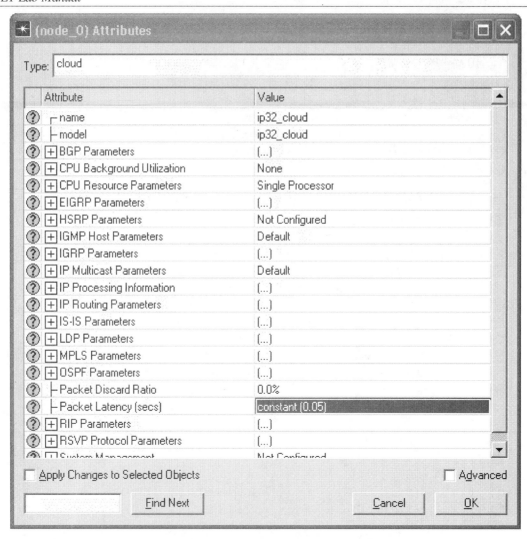

Select an **ethernet4_slip8_gtwy** device from the Object Palette and place it in the project workspace. Right click on the station and choose **View Node Description**. Note that the station supports both the Ethernet and SLIP protocols.

Right click on the station and choose **Set Name**. Set the **Name** to **Router_West**.

Click on **OK** to close the window.

Select a **10BaseT_LAN** object from the Object Palette and place it in the project workspace.

Right click on the LAN and choose **View Node Description**. Note that the LAN object represents multiple workstations and supports various applications. Click on the close window icon to close the window.

Right click on the LAN and choose **Edit Attributes**. Modify the **name** attribute of the LAN to **Home Office**. Set the **Number of Workstations** to **150**. Expand the **Application: Supported Profiles** attribute, and set the **rows** attribute to **2**. Expand the **row 0** attribute, and set the **Profile Name** to **Database_User**. Set the **Number of Clients** to **50**. Expand the **row 1** attribute and set the **Profile Name** to **Web_User**. Set the **Number of Clients** to **100**. Click on **OK** to close the window.

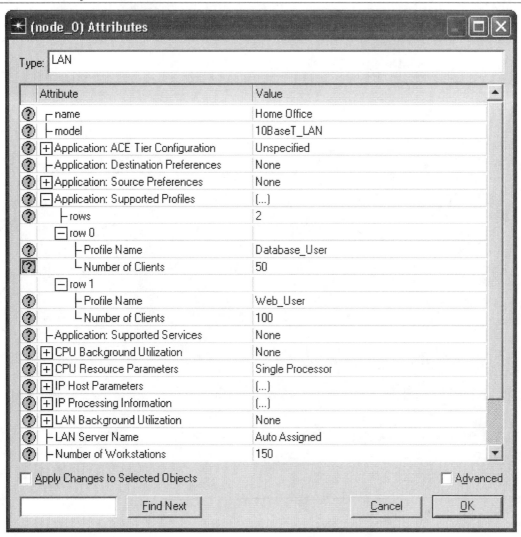

Select a **10BaseT** link from the Object Palette and use it to connect the Home Office to **Router_West**.   Select a **PPP_DS1** link from the Object Palette and use it to connect the **Router_West** to the ip32_cloud.   Remember that DS1 speed is 1.5 Mbps.

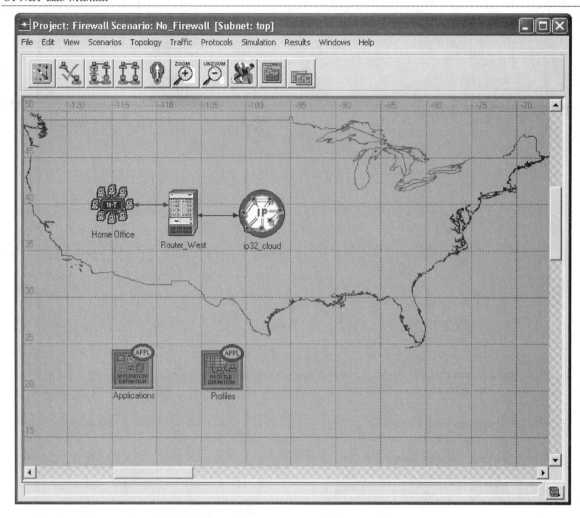

We have completed configuring the client side. Now we need to build the server side.

Select an **ethernet4_slip8_gtwy** device from the Object Palette and place it in the project workspace. Right click on the station and choose **Set Name**. Set the **Name** to **Router_East**. Click on **OK** to close the window.

Select a **ppp_server** device from the Object Palette and place two copies in the project workspace. Right click on the first server and choose **Edit Attributes**. Set the **name** to **Database Server**. Edit the **Application: Supported Services** attribute, and set the number of **rows** to **1**. Edit the **Name** field of the first row and set to **Database Access (Heavy)**. Click on **OK** twice to close the windows.

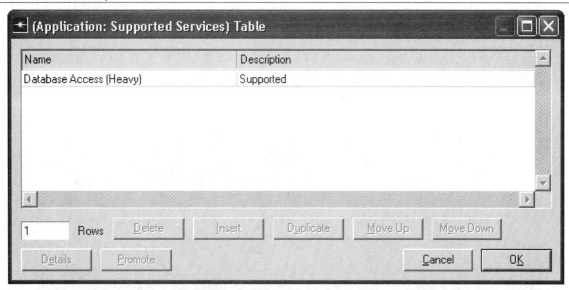

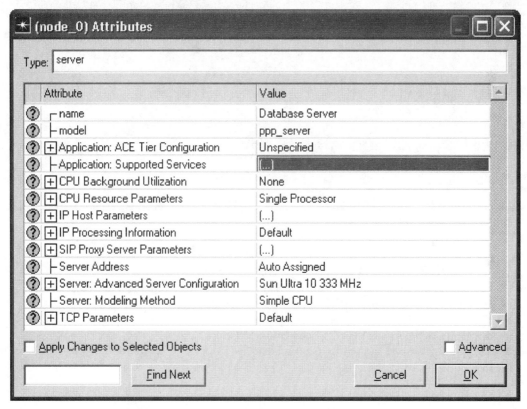

Right click on the second server and choose **Edit Attributes**. Set the **name** to **Web Server**. Edit the **Application: Supported Services** attribute, and set the number of **rows** to **1**. Edit the **Name** field of the first row and set to **Web Browsing (Heavy HTTP1.1)**. Click on **OK** twice to close the windows.

Select two **PPP_DS3** links from the Object Palette and use them to connect the Database Server to **Router_East**, and the Web Server to **Router_East**. Select a **PPP_DS1** link and use it to connect **Router_East** to the ip32_cloud.

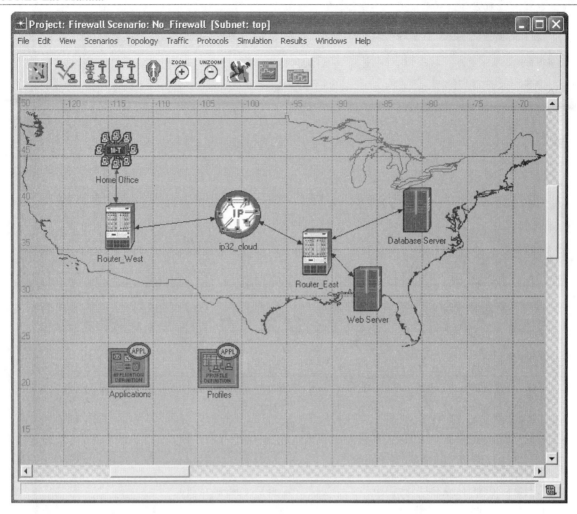

Configure the Simulation

Select the **Simulation** tab => **Choose Individual Statistics...**
Expand the **Global Statistics** item and the **DB Query** item, and select the **Response Time (sec)** statistic.
Expand the **HTTP** item and select the **Page Response Time (seconds)** statistic.
Expand the **Node Statistics** item and the **Server DB Query** item, and select the **Load (requests/sec)**.
Expand the **Server HTTP** item and select the **Load (requests/sec).**
Expand the **Link Statistics** and the **point-to-point** item, and select the **utilization <--** and **utilization -->** statistics.
Click on **OK** to close window.

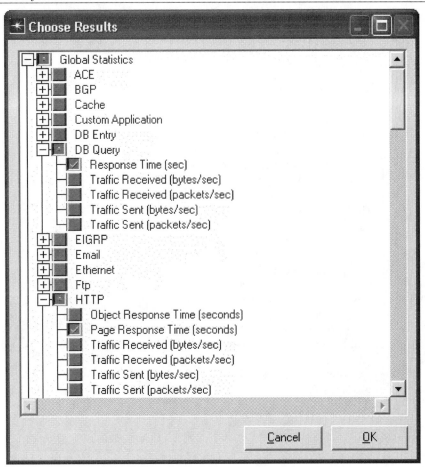

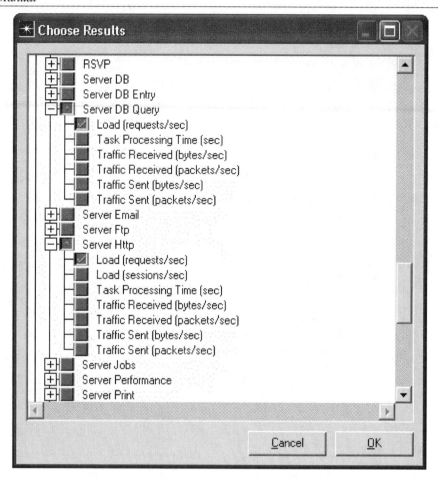

Select **Simulation => Configure Discrete Event Simulation...**
Under the **Common** tab, set the **Duration** to **200**, and the unit to **second(s)**.
Click on **OK** to close the window.

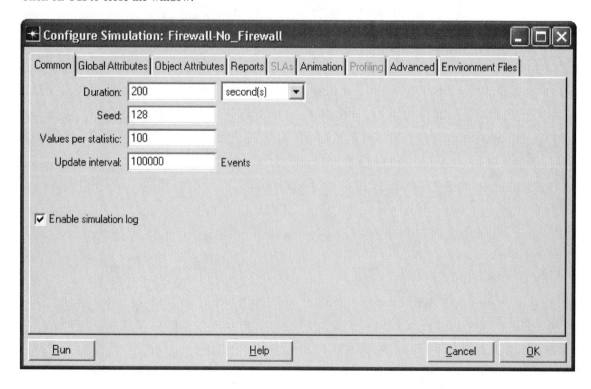

Duplicate the Scenario

We are now going to duplicate the scenario to model a network with a firewall replacing **Router_West**. We will create one scenario in which the firewall allows traffic through, but adds processing delay due to the packet filtering required. We will create another scenario in which the firewall discards web traffic. This will allow us to compare the database performance application in these different instances.

Choose **Scenarios => Duplicate Scenario**, and name the new scenario **Firewall**.

Right click on **Router_West**, and choose **Edit Attributes**. Edit the **model** and choose **ethernet2_slip8_firewall** from the pull-down menu. Expand the **Proxy Server Information** attribute and the **row 1** attribute (which describes the Database Proxy behavior). Set the **Latency** to **constant(0.005)**. Expand the **row 4** attribute (which describes the HTTP Proxy behavior) and set the **Latency** to **constant(0.005)**. Note that both applications show **Proxy Server Deployed** set to **yes**. This means that the firewall will allow traffic generated by these two applications to pass through.
Click on **OK** to close the window and replace the gateway with the firewall.

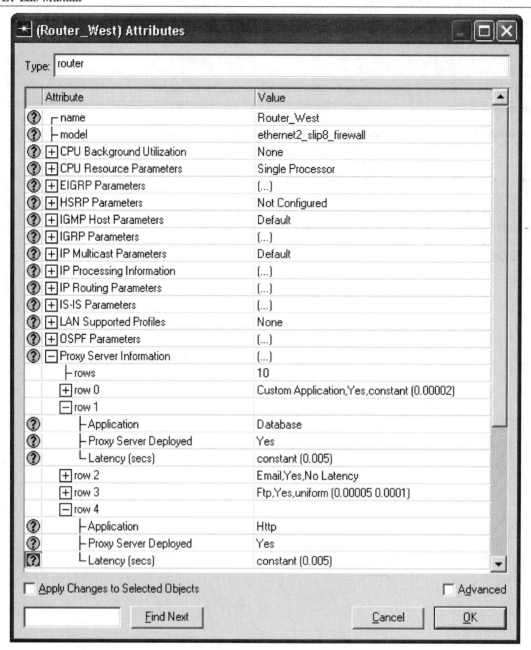

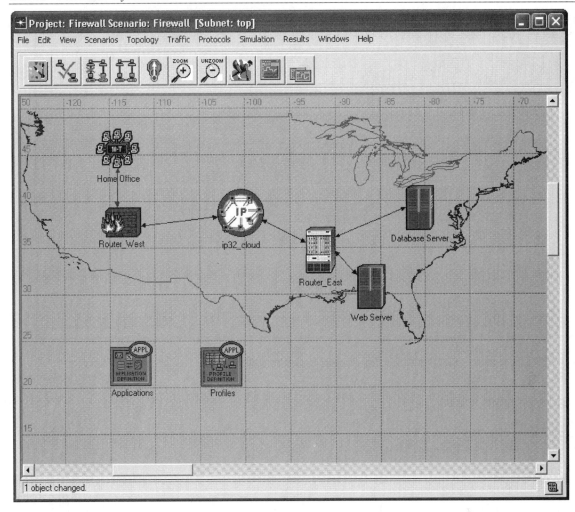

Choose **Scenarios** => **Duplicate Scenario** again, and name the new scenario **Firewall_Blocking**.

Right click on **Router_West**, and choose **Edit Attributes**. Expand the **Proxy Server Information** attribute, and the **row 4** attribute (which describes the HTTP Proxy behavior). Set the **Proxy Server Deployed** attribute to **no**. This means that the firewall will discard all web traffic.
Click on **OK** to close the window.

Run the Simulation

Select the **Scenarios** tab => **Manage Scenarios...**
Edit the **Results** field for all three rows and set the value to **<collect>** or **<recollect>**.
Click on **OK** to run the scenarios (one after the other).

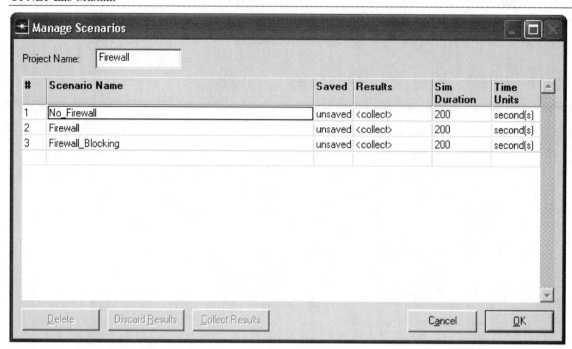

When the simulation has completed, click on **Close** to close the window.

Inspect and Analyze Results

Select the **Scenarios** tab => **Switch to Scenario.** Switch to the **No_Firewall** scenario.
Select the **Results** tab => **Compare Results...**

Expand the **Global Statistics** item and the **DB Query** item, and select the **Response Time (sec)** statistic. This statistic shows how long each database query took to complete. Use **average** mode to view the statistic. Click on **Show** to see a more detailed graph. You can see that adding the firewall increased response time significantly due to the proxy-processing latency that the firewall imposed. When the web traffic was filtered out, the database response time went back down, since it was not competing for bandwidth with the web traffic. Click on the close window icon and choose to **Delete** the panel. Click on the statistic again to disable the preview.

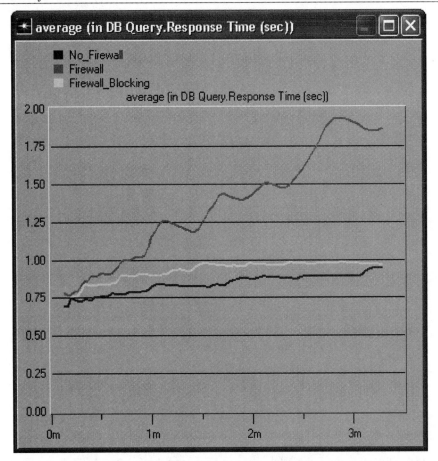

Expand the **HTTP** item and select the **Page Response Time (seconds)** statistic.   View the statistic using **average** mode.   Click on **Show**. There is no line for the **Firewall_Blocking** scenario since no web requests were completed.   You can see that, again, the addition of the firewall greatly increased the response time. Click on the close window icon and choose to **Delete** the panel.   Click on the statistic again to disable the preview.

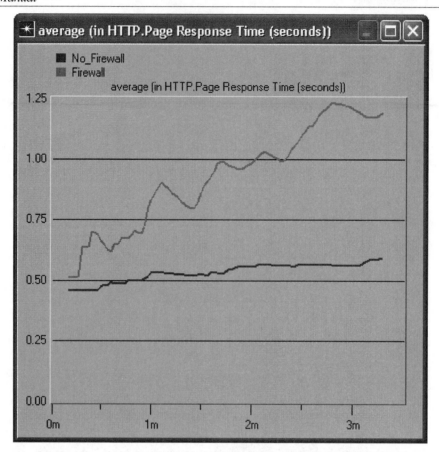

Expand the **Object Statistics** item, the **Web Server** item, and the **Server HTTP** item. Select the **Load (requests/sec)** statistic and use **average** mode to view the statistic. Click on **Show**. Note that the web server load goes to zero when filtering is done by the firewall (in the **Firewall_Blocking** scenario). Click on the close window icon and choose to **Delete** the panel. Click on the statistic again to disable the preview.

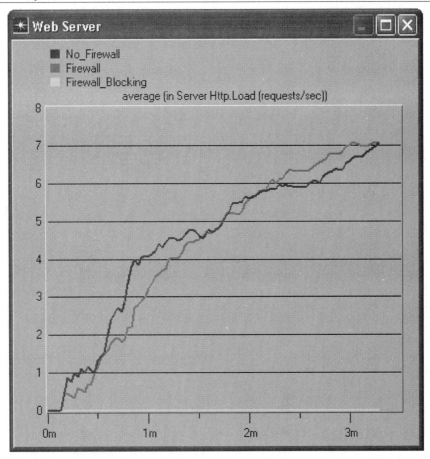

Expand the **Router_West <-> ip32_cloud[0]** item, and the **point-to-point** item, and select the **utilization -->** statistic. Use **average** mode to view the statistic.   Click on **Show**. This statistic shows the amount of traffic that was seen on the DS1 link between **Router_West** and the WAN. You can see that the lowest utilization corresponds to the **Firewall_Blocking** scenario due to the removal of the web traffic requests. Click on the close window icon and choose to **Delete** the panel. Click on **Close** to close the **Compare Results** window.

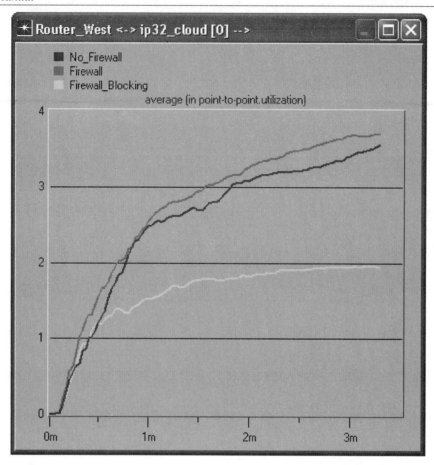

Save your model and close all windows.

Questions

1. Firewalls can often act as bottlenecks if they are unable to forward packets at the same rate that they receive them. Duplicate the Firewall scenario and name it **Firewall_Latency**. Edit the Proxy attributes of the firewall, and set the latency for the Database application to constant(0). Rerun the simulation and record the DB Query Response Time. Repeat for values of 0.002, 0.004, 0.006, and 0.008. Graph your values and explain your results.

2. Calculate the amount of traffic generated by one database user. Use the parameters set in **the Database Access (Heavy)** application description. Now calculate the total load from all the database users (there are 50). Do the same calculations for the **Web Browsing (Heavy HTTP1.1)** application. Examine the Web Server load and Database Server load statistics from the three scenarios described in the lab. Do the results match your calculated load? Why or why not? You may also want to look at the global DB Query and HTTP Traffic Sent statistics.

3. Switch to the Firewall scenario and edit the attributes of **Router_West**. Expand the Proxy Server Information attribute. For each of the applications listed, explain whether incoming traffic destined for this application should be filtered or not. Explain your answer. Repeat for outgoing traffic.

5283 -
Kingsbury way